Inspired Nurse

by Rich Bluni, RN

Published by:
Fire Starter Publishing
913 Gulf Breeze Parkway, Suite 6
Gulf Breeze, FL 32561
Phone: 850-934-1099
Fax: 850-934-1384
www.firestarterpublishing.com

Cover Design by Cassandra Henze

ISBN: 978-0-9749986-7-1

Library of Congress Control Number: 2009921394

The stories in this book are true. However, names and identifying details have been changed to protect the privacy of all concerned.

Printed in the United States of America

DEDICATION

This book is dedicated to:

My beautiful wife, Dawn, an awesome nurse. You inspire me every day and I love you. I am very blessed to be on this journey with you.

My son, Rhett. You are the joy of my life. I am so proud to be your dad.

My soon-to-be-born son, Luke. I can't wait to meet you.

Nurses everywhere. Thank you for doing what you do. You are remarkable.

Studer Group team. You are all my heroes.

Quint Studer. You are the best thing to happen to healthcare since penicillin! Thank you for lighting my fire.

WRITE YOUR WAY TO INSPIRATION

Inspired JOURNAL

Your work as a nurse brings many inspiring moments. By setting aside time to explore and reflect on these events in writing, you can more fully integrate their gifts into your daily life.

Inspired Journal was created to help you do just that. Perhaps it was packaged with your copy of *Inspired Nurse*. If so, please use it as you complete the "spiritual stretches" at the end of each chapter in the book.

If you purchased the book you're holding separately, and wish to order a copy of *Inspired Journal*, please visit www.studergroup.com or www.firestarterpublishing.com.

Writing is a powerful tool for spiritual and emotional growth. Give it a try. The life you enrich may be your own.

TABLE OF CONTENTS

FOREWORD

Nurses are brave. Insightful. Compassionate. Not only do they help people heal, they calm fears, alleviate grief, inspire others. To be a nurse is to answer a calling to tireless service and self-sacrifice.

Every nurse has paid a price for his or her dedication. As rewarding as it is to touch lives on such a profound emotional and spiritual level, it can also be stressful and heartbreaking. It's a tough, tough job...and that's why it's so important to make sure nurses are nurtured.

Inspired Nurse offers a reminder of what a difference nurses make. Rich Bluni has set forth an incredible "journey of inspiration"—a journey that I hope will help you reconnect (or stay connected) to the sense of purpose that brought you to this calling.

Please share this book and its accompanying journal with others you feel would benefit from or enjoy them.

The work you do is so meaningful. Thank you.

Quint Studer, CEO
Studer Group

INTRODUCTION

PART I: THE PURPOSE OF THIS BOOK

Most nurses, when we first begin our journey, could hardly feel more inspired. Being a nurse is the very *definition* of inspiring. After all, our work saves lives. It helps sick people heal. Nurses are present at those sacred moments when patients leave this world and those joyful moments when new life enters it. We ease pain. We help patients and the people who love them get through some of the toughest challenges they will ever face.

It's a privilege to touch lives in such profound ways.

That's what most of us are thinking on our first day at the hospital or medical practice or home healthcare agency. And it's true. There *is* something special, something life-affirming and awe inspiring, about being a nurse.

Problem is, it's not always easy to sustain that feeling. Roadblocks rise up under your feet and deplete the energy that once fueled your journey. Real life creeps in. Your "new nurse" idealism starts to fray under the reality of paperwork and red tape and grumpy coworkers and aching feet and just plain too much work to ever get done in one shift.

Patients stop looking like opportunities to make a powerful human connection—to make a difference in someone's life—and start looking like just one more bedpan or vital sign or test or painkiller prescription. You get tired. You begin to burn out.

Sure, it's probably like this at other jobs. But you don't want to think of nursing as just "a job." It's a calling. The stakes are higher. You know that in your heart. So why can't you remember it, 24/7?

Well, because you're human and because this is one of the toughest professions in the world. (So the first order of business is: Forgive yourself!)

The good news—no, the *great* news—is that you can reconnect to that inspired feeling, even if you've been a nurse for five years or thirty years. You know this already. Sometimes a patient comes along who touches you on a deep "soul" level and reminds you why you chose this work.

Those moments don't have to be rare and isolated and fleeting. You can make a choice to a) live in the present and become mindful of the opportunities that happen all around you, b) hold onto those moments of inspiration and integrate them into your daily life, and c) share them with others in your life.

And that's the purpose of this book. Each chapter begins with a story that demonstrates my own journey to inspired nurse-dom. It then segues into a section titled *Inspiration Destination*—a section that contains a couple of "spiritual stretches" based on the lesson I learned that you can put into practice.

Don't worry. These "stretches" are nothing too complicated. Mostly, they're calls to reflect on your own experiences and to take some simple, yet meaningful action that moves you a step further along on your journey to being an inspired nurse.

I'd like to encourage you to keep a journal as you work your way through this book. It's amazing how much you can learn about yourself through the simple act of putting pen to paper.

Of course, I know you have a busy, busy life. (Do I *ever* know!) You're unlikely to have the time or inclination to pore over this book and put every spiritual stretch into practice. It's okay. A journey of a thousand miles begins with a single step, as some wise person once said.

So please—embrace the Inspiration Destinations and make the stretches doable for your lifestyle. You're looking to become more inspired and that's a very personal process.

While you can certainly take this journey solo, there are other ways to use *Inspired Nurse*. You may choose to challenge your friends, team, staff, colleagues, department, division, unit, council, faculty, committee, hospital, system, or entire organization to go on these "Inspiration Destinations" together.

Imagine the force of nature and the tidal wave of inspiration that you could create! Imagine an entire hospital, system, or school committing to inspiring themselves and others! Wouldn't that be awesome?

Inspiration fuels passion. Passion encourages action. Action changes the world.

PART II: THE DAY I ASKED "THE QUESTION"

Why am I doing this? That's The Question. Sooner or later, all nurses ask it.

It's good to ask questions. It is, after all, what smart people do.

I remember when I asked The Question for the first time. I was in my late twenties and working in a busy Pediatric Intensive Care Unit. In my time there, I held the hands of many dying children and their parents. I saw valiant struggles, brave battles, and heartbreaking losses. It was, and remains, the toughest job I have ever had. The team members I worked alongside were, and are still, my heroes. I may not have been the best among them, but I was among the best for sure.

What led me to question my life's path was a little girl. She was brought to us clinging to life. Her mother's boyfriend had beaten her mercilessly for the simple transgression of eating his French fries. She was small, frail, and helpless. Her mother was in jail. I do not recall any family, only the kind lawyer who was her court-appointed guardian.

The court agreed to remove her from life support. She was deemed brain-dead. I had only recently become a dad, so this felt different from the other children who had come before. It hit closer to home.

As we began the process of disconnecting her and administering medications, we all looked knowingly at each other, communicating in that silent way nurses do when they have worked together for awhile. We all knew that she deserved to be surrounded by love in these last moments.

I wrapped a blanket around her, lifted her from the bed, cradled her in my arms, and sat down in a rocking chair. We closed the curtain around the bed. The physician, a wonderful young woman who also recently became a parent, and several of the other nurses all gathered around. Quietly. Respectfully. I don't know why I did it, but I began singing "Somewhere Over the Rainbow." It was the song I sang to my infant son to lull him to sleep.

I doubt anyone had ever sung this little girl a song, or rocked her to sleep. Certainly not her unknown father. Certainly not the animal that did this to her. The old cigarette burn marks, bruises, and scars spread out all over her small body told a different story, not of lullabies but of nightmares. I sang to her. Quietly. Respectfully. I don't remember if the others sang along. I think they might have. I cried. They cried. Her heartrate slowed, her breathing slowed. She died in my arms.

We all touched her as if to give to her that which she never had. She was not the first child I saw leave this world and she would not be the last, but I remember her. Having a four-year-old die in your arms is tough. It was then that I asked The Question for the first time: *Why am I doing this?*

Have you asked that question? I am sure that you have. Probably a few hundred times if your career has been long enough. I could never come up with the answer until I began working with Studer Group®. Quint Studer, the founder of Studer Group, summed it up for me in a few simple words: *Purpose, Worthwhile Work and Making a Difference.* That is why we do this. That is why I did this.

I work as a coach and a speaker with Studer Group now. I no longer hold the hands of dying children or ride in the back of ambulances or pray at the bedside with scared families or loved ones. My work has changed, but my love for those who still teach nurses, work at the bedside, or lead those that do, remains.

I hear their stories everywhere I travel. They are passionate, these nurses. They give so much. They are nurses twenty-four hours a day, seven days a week. This book is for them, for you. I pray that it will touch you, make you smile, and maybe inspire you. I hope you read on.

CHAPTER

INSPIRATION DESTINATION:
TEN MINUTES OF PURPOSE

THE DAY THE NURSE STOOD STILL

I saw it happen in my mind before it happened. Have you ever had that experience? You hear or think something and then a second later it actually happens? I was driving home from work and I saw a car flipping over in my mind. I saw that it was a silver Honda. It was that clear of a premonition. I always believed that stuff like that really happened but just not to me. Then it happened.

I looked across the median at the southbound traffic as I was headed north on a fairly busy I-95 in South Florida. I saw a car go airborne and begin flipping. I remember a piece of black plastic hitting my car. My heart was pounding. *This couldn't be good.*

I pulled over, got out, jumped the guardrail and sprinted to the car. It was wheels-down, crushed and smoking. A young mother emerged from the driver side screaming, "My baby!" Onlookers approached the car and some recoiled and began screaming things like, "Oh my God, the baby is dead!" I didn't know what I would find. I think I pushed some gawkers away and probably told people that I was a nurse. It was like I was watching the scene unfold from outside of my body, like a movie. I was scared. *Really* scared. If you have ever been in this situation, you know what I mean.

I think I stood perfectly still for one second while my brain re-booted. The child's mother was trying to open the door. There was a lot of noise: voices, traffic, and of course the car's running engine. I heard the word "go" in my head and I took action. I moved the mom and was able to pull open the mangled door. I called out to a guy in the crowd to shut the engine off, and he did.

There she was. The little girl in the car looked to be about three years old. She was in her carseat in the back. There was blood everywhere and she was not moving—or breathing. Her pulse was barely evident.

A lot happened in those few seconds. I knew I had to get her breathing. I could feel her life leaving her body. As I tried to fit into the crushed doorway while simultaneously stabilizing her C-spine and opening her airway, I didn't notice the broken glass stabbing into my leg. I couldn't hear the onlookers screaming. It was just the two of us.

I felt woefully unprepared for this. When I opened her airway, it seemed as if a cup of blood poured forth. I had no gloves. I had no mouthpiece. But what I did have was a dying baby. I prayed and I quickly wiped her mouth and gave her some breaths. Her mom was trying to get to her, but a kind lady grabbed her tightly and said, "He's trying to help."

More blood.

I gave her some more breaths, and then suddenly the little girl gasped for air and moaned. I held her airway open and I could feel her pulse pick up again. "Thank you," I said to Heaven.

My leg ached from the metal and glass stabbing me. My back and neck were cramping from the awkward position, but you couldn't have moved me from that little girl with a crowbar. I heard the welcomed sounds of the approaching Fire Rescue team—the heroes who do this stuff every day.

They were everywhere all at once. I began rattling off a "report" on what had happened. "Are you a paramedic?" asked one of the paramedics. I said, "No, I'm a nurse." He said, "You just saved this kid, buddy."

We stabilized her C-spine, kept her airway open, and gave her some oxygen. She was only semi-conscious, but she was breathing and moving. The paramedic asked me, "How badly are you hurt?" I was covered in blood and looked so stunned at that point, that he thought I was the driver. Before I could speak, a witness began telling the paramedic what had happened and my role in what transpired. I could only nod in agreement at the witness's description. I think I was in shock.

As the rescue workers treated the mother, I could hear her yelling, "Thank you! Thank you!" The paramedic smiled at me and asked if I wanted a towel and if he could look at my leg. I saw myself in the window of a State Trooper's car. I had blood all over my face, hands, and clothing, and my leg had a small gash. The State Trooper asked me questions about what I saw. It was then that I realized that my legs were shaking so hard I thought there was an earthquake. I was now a gasping, shaking, adrenaline-crashing mess.

I sat down on the wall. The kind Florida State Trooper put his hand on my shoulder and smiled. "That's your adrenaline coming down. It happens to me sometimes after I chase a suspect." I thought that was nice of him to say. I must have looked pathetic. I think I shook all the way home. I am in awe of people who do those types of things every day.

A lot happened after that. The family got my information from the State Trooper and contacted the press. I met the family and even went over to their house for dinner. It was one of the most inspiring things that has ever happened to me.

I have talked to many nurses and other healthcare professionals who have had experiences similar to mine. Most of them talked about how calm they were during the event but then "crashed," as I did, afterwards. Not one of them thought twice before they jumped in the water, climbed in the burning car, or performed CPR in the movie theater.

How fortunate I was to have been at the right place at the right time. Thank goodness for the paramedics, firefighters, and others who have a roadside or a twisted piece of metal as their "bed-space" every day as they care for their patients. I certainly was an unlikely roadside Good Samaritan. The most heroic thing I had ever done on a roadside was to change my own flat tire once. I also forgot to tighten some of the bolts and the spare fell off as I drove back onto the highway. Pretty impressive, huh?

There have been occasions since that day where I have felt discouraged as a nurse and needed to be reminded of why I do this. I have the newspaper story about me and the little girl framed on my home office wall. A wonderful coworker gave it to me as a gift. Every once in a while, I read it. I relive the accident and some of the scary moments, but mostly

I remember the very moment when that baby took a breath. I can feel her heartbeat start to kick in and I get that rush of joy all over again.

This story isn't meant to portray me as a hero. I'm not bragging. Quite the contrary. This is a story about a time when a fellow nurse was reminded that he made a difference. It was my most inspiring moment. What is yours?

Sometimes we need to remind ourselves that what we do each day, with every patient, is inspiring. Even though there are times when the tires do come off, there are many more times when we make a difference.

INSPIRATION DESTINATION: TEN MINUTES OF PURPOSE.

SPIRITUAL STRETCH #1: Before leaving your house for work today, allow for ten extra minutes. Get up earlier, shut off the T.V., and ask the family to give you some "me" time. Sit someplace peaceful and quiet. If you need to do this on the bus, or train, that's fine too. Just be sure to carve out that ten minutes.

During this time, think about an occasion when you felt that you made a difference as a nurse—an occasion in which you felt connected to your purpose. Perhaps think of this moment as your "most inspiring nursing experience ever."

Remember that patient who told you that you were her "angel"? Or that family member who called you her "knight in shining armor"? That time where you made the difference between life and death, when you saw a nursing student of yours have an "ah-ha moment" or an employee of yours blossom into a high performer under your mentorship? How did that feel?

Now, close your eyes and relive that experience. Remember the sounds and the sights. Hear the voices. Hear the monitor bells; see the defibrillator reach its charge. Get back there. Your goal is to recreate the whole experience for yourself.

Embrace the feeling of purpose. Feel the sense of pride, of accomplishment. Your mind doesn't know the difference between it really happening and the memory. Feel that inspiration. Feel all the feelings that you felt. The joy. The spirit. Stay there for several minutes.

This may take practice, but it is a powerful exercise. Relive your shining moment as a nurse. When was the day that you "stood still"? When did you feel like you could fly?

When your ten minutes are up, open your eyes. How do you feel? If you haven't felt close to your purpose for a while, this is a good way to get started. Use this exercise to prepare for your shift, or your lecture, or your nursing management meeting. This is far superior to starting your day with anxiety or dread over your assignments, deadlines, or patients.

Carry this relived experience throughout your day. When you feel discouraged, find 30 seconds to bring the images from your ten minutes of purpose back into your mind. This is a powerful use of a short amount of time. Do this as often as you like. And don't be surprised if your list of "inspiring moments" begins to grow.

You're on the way to being an inspired nurse.

SPIRITUAL STRETCH #2: Think about these pivotal times in your work. How were you "different" then? Are there days where inspiration is right in front of you? What does the following sentence mean to you: *Look for reasons to be inspired.*

Journal your inspiration. Write the "good" stories. They may not have had happy endings, but perhaps your experience was an eyeopener or motivated you to be better. Such moments make all the difference.

CHAPTER

INSPIRATION DESTINATION:
HONOR YOUR MENTOR

TWO PLUS TWO = FIVE

I wasn't able to start nursing school when I had hoped and it was because of my old worst enemy. Math. I just am not a math person. I still count on my fingers and need a calculator for the simplest equations. Now, math would be the reason I was going to have to wait a year to start school. That is, until I met Jackie.

Jackie was one of the teachers at the nursing school I hoped to attend. She told me that she would help me pass the test that would meet my math requirement for school. Frankly, I thought I had a better chance of picking the winning lotto tickets 27 times in a row, but hey, what did I have to lose?

It was not easy, and I'm not sure Jackie realized what she had gotten herself into. I studied for hours a day and met with her at least twice a week for tutoring, practice tests, and review sessions. I needed an 85 percent on the test to gain entrance into the program. I doubted it was possible. However, she never doubted me for a second.

Why did this matter so much to her? She did not know me or have any connection to me, but for some reason, she cared. She worked with me in her spare time and even coached me via the telephone. She made me work harder than I had ever worked before.

The day of the test arrived. I was more than nervous—actually I felt like the weight of the world was on my shoulders. It was make or break time. I prayed, did deep breathing, and paced. Meanwhile, Jackie came walking down the hall with a big smile on her face. "You can do this; you have come so far," she said to me. At least one of us felt confident.

She sat in her office closely monitoring me from a few feet away while I took the test. The buzzer went off and my time was up. She took my test, put her hand on my shoulder and asked me to wait in the hallway as she graded it. Time crawled. Jackie emerged from her office with the test in her hands, and I couldn't read her face.

"Well, Mr. Bluni, you got a 92 percent. Congratulations, we will see you in January." I couldn't believe what I just heard. Maybe she made a mistake? I had never received better than a "C" on anything math-related. What an awesome teacher she was! There was just no way I could have done this without her. I stood up and hugged her. I could barely get out the words "Thank you."

Jackie's support changed my life. What if I hadn't started that year? Would I have moved onto something else, become discouraged, given up on nursing? I know I thanked her but I don't know if she really knew how much it meant to me.

Now here's the best part of this story. (This should give hope to all of you who are "mathematically disenfranchised" like me.) During nursing school, I became a student tutor for pharmacology math! No, really! Jackie had not only helped me to better understand a difficult subject, she had given me confidence where I had none. This helped me to be able to work with others who struggled with math. I could relate to them. We all counted on our fingers together.

Jackie passed away a few years ago. I felt that loss in my heart when I heard the sad news, even though I had not seen her in more than a decade. I wish I had the chance to say to her one more time, "Thank you, Jackie. You did more for me than you will ever know."

INSPIRATION DESTINATION: HONOR YOUR MENTOR.

SPIRITUAL STRETCH #1: Who first suggested nursing school to you? Who did you cry to during your exams? Who was your best preceptor? Who was that manager who insisted, "You can do this!" when you thought for sure that you could not? Who was that nursing instructor who amazed you with a combination of heart, brains, and caring? Who was that experienced nurse who took you under her wing and showed you the ropes?

Think where you would be without any one of these people. Imagine how much more difficult your job would be without the foundation that they helped create. To butcher Janet Jackson's lyrics: "What have you done for them lately?" Seriously, have you ever really thanked your mentors for the difference that they have made in your life? When was the last time you called them? Took them out or sent a card? Or just told them how very important they were and are to you?

Why not make some time to do something for your mentors and let them know the difference that they have made, or continue to make, in your life? This can be as simple or extravagant as you want. Just make it real and heartfelt.

There is much value to honoring our mentors. They, after all, are people like us. They struggle with doubt and fear. They question and lose their way. What better gift to give than the gift of gratitude?

This is a gift that will serve two purposes. When you honor a mentor and share with her the difference she has made in your life, you will relive the feelings of being inspired and the moments you grew the most. At the same time, you may inspire your mentor to give others the same gift that she gave you. You may even inspire yourself to become a mentor.

Honoring your mentor may open a door that has been long closed and let in the fresh fragrant air of inspiration—for both of you!

Perhaps your mentor is no longer of this world. This exercise can still be a powerful one. Write him a letter, as if he were here for you to hand it to him. If he is buried somewhere, get some flowers, roll up your letter, tie a ribbon around it and bring it to his gravesite. Spend some time there, silently meditate, or pray. Give thanks for all that he's done. If there is no memorial site for your mentor, go to someplace that was meaningful to or representative of him and talk to him. Give him thanks. You may believe that he hears you, or you may not. That's okay. This is for you.

Honoring your mentor is meant to serve as a reminder that there are people along the way who have made this journey possible, meaningful, and even beautiful. You are here today because of them. Let them know that, wherever they are.

SPIRITUAL STRETCH #2: Where would you be without your mentor? Write the qualities, in single adjectives, that describe him or her. They may be "honest" or "smart" or "empathetic." Put them somewhere where you can read them every day. Think about what these words mean to you in your journey as a nurse. What have you learned from your mentor that you can use to mentor others?

CHAPTER

INSPIRATION DESTINATION:
THANK A FAMILY MEMBER OR FRIEND FOR HIS OR HER SUPPORT

ROCKET MAN

My dad was a cool guy. He was exactly what a dad is supposed to be. He came from a very different generation and sometimes had ways very different from my own. Still, I always knew a few things for certain. One was that my dad loved me. I don't know if he said it often, but there was no doubt in my mind that he did.

Also, my dad was proud of me. I was fortunate enough to have had some success in high school within the performing arts. My dad never missed a show, and he was usually early to ensure that he got a good seat. I learned later that he bragged about me to all of his friends. That meant a lot.

Dad wasn't the type to sit on the sidelines and nail you whenever you messed up. He would quietly nod at you as if to say "It's okay, kid, you'll get it." He could be tough, but I always knew he had my back. I felt safe when he was around.

He was a maintenance foreman at a large hospital in Miami. He loved his job. I never heard him complain about work or his coworkers. I think he may have called in sick only once in over twenty years, and that was because my mom threatened his life if he didn't! He was solid.

As a kid, I had the sound of his car memorized and I knew when he was pulling up the block from work. We weren't some perfect T.V. family. My dad didn't come home from work, swing me up on his shoulders, and take me out for ice cream every night. He didn't need to. He just had a presence about him, and as a kid I thought he could do no wrong.

At the age of fifty-eight, my dad was diagnosed with prostate cancer. I was around twenty-two years old. I had just moved back to Miami from New York and wasn't sure what I was going to be when I grew up.

My dad was in the hospital quite a bit, and I spent much time with him there. He would frequently point out to me that I would make a good nurse, adding that the hospital where he worked had a scholarship program that would pay for my schooling since I was a child of an employee.

In other words, he planted the seed. Many nurses encouraged me, as well. I grew close to them as my family and I practically lived in the hospital during this time. One nurse in particular helped me get my start in school and was very supportive at the start of my journey. I am grateful to her for that.

Anyway, I started school and I loved it. It was the hardest challenge I had ever undertaken in my young life, but it was worth it. I remember taking my microbiology class at night. The class ended at 8 p.m. Visiting hours at the hospital where my dad was admitted also ended at 8 p.m.

I drove right past the hospital on my ride home, and there was no way I was going to miss the chance to see him. I perfected the art of looking like I was supposed to be in the hospital by wearing my scrubs and lab coat.

My dad got a big kick out of my "sneaking" into the hospital after hours to visit him. We had a ritual where I would bring him in a chocolate milkshake as his late-night snack. It was often the only food he would eat, as cancer and nausea wreaked havoc on his appetite.

This was a special time for us. We didn't say a lot. Sometimes I just sat there studying while he snoozed or watched television. He wasn't a talker. If you didn't know him better, you might think his silence meant he didn't want you there. Quite the contrary. Whenever I got up, he would awaken or look up and ask, "You going already?"

One night before I left, I handed him a letter I had written. It was several pages long. I told him that it was a personal letter and that he could read it later. He smiled and nodded. I kissed him on the cheek and said goodnight.

A few days went by and during one of my daytime visits my mom was there. She pulled me aside and asked me what was in the "secret letter" I had written to my dad. She told me that earlier that day she had noticed it by his bed, and when she reached for it, he snatched it out of her hand and told her, "That's personal between me and The Kid." (I was the youngest child in our family, hence the nickname.) I laughed and told her it was just a "father and son thing."

Here's the thing: I knew that my dad was going to die. I was afraid that after he died I would regret not having thanked him for something or maybe I would forget to apologize for something that I did. So in the letter I thanked him for everything he had done for me. I listed toys that he bought me and family trips we had taken. I apologized for things that I did as a teenager (yes, I was somewhat of a challenge). I thanked him for being my support and for being a true "dad." I tried to not leave anything out. I needed him to know this and I needed to have the peace of knowing that he knew it.

A few weeks later I came to visit him in his room at home, where he was being cared for by a wonderful hospice nurse. She stepped out to give us time together. He was on a lot of pain medication and was usually asleep when I visited him during those last few days. This much needed respite from the pain that he suffered was a blessing.

This day I prayed over him while holding his hand. I rested my head on his chest. I remember being very conscious of his heartbeat. It was strong. I wanted to memorize the sound. It meant he was alive. I knew that noble heart would stop soon. I wanted it to beat forever. I wanted the sound to stay in my ears.

As I stood to walk away, my dad opened his eyes and with unusual strength gripped my hand and pulled me to him. He looked me right in the eyes. My dad had the most beautiful blue eyes I have ever seen. Only my son has the same crystal blue color.

He looked at me with a sharpness that I had not seen in many weeks. He said very clearly and with laser-like focus, "I love you, Kid. You know that, right?" My dad had never said that to me. He always said, referring to my two wonderful brothers and me, "I love all of my sons." Still, he had never said it directly to me.

"Yes, Pop, I know that," I stammered. I was taken aback by not only how clear he was but how gentle his voice sounded.

"Good," he said. He smiled and went back to sleep.

Two days later I was driving home from one of my visits. I had just left my dad's bedside and as I was driving home the song "Rocket Man" by Elton John began playing on the radio. The refrain "I think it's going to be a long, long time" rang through my mind. For me, at that moment, it was a song about my dad going away and that it would be a long, long time before I would see him again. I pulled my car over and sobbed.

After several minutes I regained my composure and made it home. I walked in the door and the phone rang. It was the hospice nurse. She told me that my dad was slipping away and that I should come back.

My wife and I drove back to my parents' house in silence. To try to change the mood, my wife turned the radio on. There was nothing but commercials on and my wife was trying to find some relaxing music. She landed on a radio station and then suddenly the familiar opening bars of "Rocket Man" began to play. I had not had time to tell her about my drive home yet and my earlier reaction to the song. It felt like someone was trying to tell me something.

I pulled up to the house. The first person I saw was my oldest brother. He shook his head and looked down. I entered the room and went to my dad. I put my head on his chest. There was only silence. I tried to remember the sound of his heartbeat. I stayed there for a moment. I missed him so much. I told him I loved him and said good-bye.

It was a tough time. I knew it was inevitable but at twenty-two years old it was a lot to bear. I did have a sense of peace, though. I knew, for a fact, that my dad knew how much I appreciated all that he did for me, from toy firetrucks and walks in the Grand Canyon to helping to make nursing school possible. On the pages of that letter I wrote him was the whole story. He knew what he meant to me. I knew that he knew.

I think about him all the time. On October 11 of each year I thank him again. That was the day that wonderful heart of his stopped beating. I am so thankful that he was my dad. I am so blessed to know that he knew that.

INSPIRATION DESTINATION: THANK A FAMILY MEMBER OR FRIEND FOR HIS OR HER SUPPORT.

SPIRITUAL STRETCH #1: What family member, significant other, or friend has been a key to your nursing success? Maybe a sibling babysat your kids so you could attend class? Maybe your mom brought you dinner to your dorm room? Maybe your dad "loaned" you the money for nursing school and then as a graduation gift told you not to worry about paying him back? Maybe your friend drove you to school in the morning?

Few of us took this journey without anyone's help. Who was it who offered you support? Does she know how much you appreciate what she did for you? If she is alive, tell her. Write her, call her, bring her flowers. If she is no longer on this earth, you can still acknowledge her much like you did for your mentor.

The inspiration here does not solely lie in your loved one's reaction or in making her feel good. It dwells in the act of giving gratitude and reverence to someone who helped to make it possible for you to touch all of the lives you have touched and will touch as a nurse.

By feeding you, or paying your way, or driving you, or being a shoulder to cry on, that person made it possible for you to save lives. Give credit where credit is due. Let her know that every time you comfort the suffering, teach a new nurse, lead a team, or bring peace to the dying, she is right there with you. This will be an unforgettable experience. I promise.

SPIRITUAL STRETCH #2: If you are doing this as a team, maybe you could take this up a notch. What if you all invited your family member or friend to a dinner honoring their support? Think for a moment what that would be like! Imagine a room full of people who have supported a room full of nurses. Imagine the stories that could be told.

Imagine the inspiration.

Just make sure there's lots of tissue!

CHAPTER

4

INSPIRATION DESTINATION:

SUPPORT NEW NURSES

THE NEW KID ON THE BLOCK

These people were (and still are) amazing! How did they know all they did? It was my second week of orientation in a Pediatric Intensive Care Unit. The nurses who worked there were incredible. I was feeling a little insecure but I desperately wanted to be as good as they were.

During this time I had a complicated post-operative heart patient. I wanted to be perfect in treating him. I had a great preceptor and I wanted her to be proud of me. I did my assessment, explained the details of the procedure, answered all of her questions about the medications and even gave the update to the incoming Intensive Care Unit attending physician.

I was off to a positive start. I felt good. I was the new kid, and I was going to make it. Then I made a very different impression from the one I had planned. The patient had several lines. They were labeled with color tabs. I had to give him a small dose of Morphine. I checked, double-checked, and then accidentally pushed the medication into the arterial line rather than the venous line. Fortunately, I quickly realized my error, pulled back the fluid, stayed with and assessed my patient, and immediately alerted my preceptor and the physician.

No harm came to the patient, thank God, but I was devastated. You can't mess up on orientation, I had been told. If you did, you were out. I knew the whole staff knew what happened.

When all was well with the patient, I went into the bathroom and threw up. I also cried. I felt horrible. I had almost hurt a patient and I had lost the respect of the whole team (or so I thought). I washed my face, dried my eyes, and got back to work.

A bit later my preceptor came over with the attending physician and the charge nurse. This was it. I tried to look calm but I knew what was coming. *Maybe I deserved it* I thought. *Maybe I am not good enough to work here.* So many thoughts raced through my mind.

"Rich, we know how you must feel," my preceptor began. "I can see it in your eyes. We were all talking about how you handled yourself and we respect how you put your patient first, called it what it was, and took ownership. We have all made mistakes, but it is what you do once you've made one that shows what kind of nurse you are.

"Now, we'll talk about how to take steps to prevent a repeat," she continued. "We need to talk with the patient's parents as well, and I want to go over everything with you so that you can learn from this. Understand, this was a serious error. You have to be on your toes 100 percent of the time in here, and it cannot happen again. All that being said, you earned our respect today. We wanted you to know that..."

Frankly, this was not what I expected. Being a new nurse who had made a big mistake, I thought I would be cast out forever. Yet instead of feeling destroyed, I felt inspired and supported. I still was devastated over the fact that I almost harmed a patient, but I was now more committed than ever to ensuring that never happened again.

I studied harder, focused more, checked and triple-checked, asked for training, and worked hard. Eventually, I made it off of orientation and was fortunate enough to work there for several years and became a preceptor myself. I learned to do my best among the best. I still stand in awe of that team. They could have written me off but instead they lifted me up. What a blessing.

Still, I've never forgotten the challenges that face a new nurse. I can still remember the knots in my stomach that seemed to last throughout my entire orientation period. There were so many times I felt like giving up.

This may have been true for you during your journey as a new nurse, as well. I was lucky. Time and time again, I was offered support, mentoring, understanding, and friendship by people I aspired (and still aspire) to emulate. I learned so much from them. They were and are amazing nurses, and I am so grateful to have had the honor to work among them.

INSPIRATION DESTINATION: SUPPORT NEW NURSES.

SPIRITUAL STRETCH #1: Think back to when you were "the new nurse." It was surely a challenge being new. Being the new *anything* can be a challenge. It seems everyone knows everything already, and the simplest tasks take you five times longer than they do everyone else.

Remember looking around for that friendly face, kind smile, and patient voice? When you found that, it was a place of rest, a sanctuary from the fear and self-doubt that sometimes felt like it may smother you.

Today, find a new or newer nurse on duty. Take a minute to stop and talk to him. Never underestimate how much this may mean to him. This shouldn't be a "drive-by" conversation either. Make it something real and substantive. Invite him to lunch. Ask him to come on break with you, or join you for a cup of coffee.

Let this nurse know that you remember what it was like to be new, and that you are willing to help anytime it is needed. Invite him into your "circle." If there is a group of seasoned nurses who go to lunch together, for instance, invite the newer nurse along for the ride.

Doing this serves several purposes. First, you will help a new nurse to feel welcome. If you receive any comments from your peers that are less than positive, remind them that such efforts to retain new nurses not only encourages their fellow professionals, but that the added staff makes vacation times, holidays, and weekends easier to bear for all!

Second, you will break through the unhealthy cliques that can develop, sometimes quite by accident. We don't always realize that we exclude others. I have seen many examples of new nurses feeling "left out" and it was not because anyone meant to make them feel that way. It was often just "how things were" on that unit. Opening up the cliques allows for new ideas and even can create new friends and better working relationships.

Remember what it was like to be the new kid on the block? I sure do. Can you find a way to smooth the path for someone else? Who knows what that simple gesture may bring to harvest in the future.

SPIRITUAL STRETCH #2: Mentors and teachers who take new nurses under their wings can make a big difference. Ask yourself, *What three things do I wish someone would have said to or done for me when I was just starting out?* Write them down. Now...do them for or say them to a new nurse. Wasn't that easy? It is very inspiring to be inspiring, isn't it?

CHAPTER 5

INSPIRATION DESTINATION:
NOTICE THE MIRACULOUS

TO DREAM OF ANGELS

It was a quiet night, and those were rare indeed. I had been a nurse for only a year or so, but I knew even then that I wasn't supposed to say the "Q" word. (Tempting fate, and all.) But I can say it safely now.

One reason peaceful nights were hard to come by was because we were working in a large academic center. Another was because the folks we were caring for were teenagers. They could be a rowdy bunch, but they were a blast. The night would have not been memorable, beyond being uncharacteristically quiet, had it not taken a most surprising turn.

Ben was a seventeen-year-old heart transplant patient. He was quick with a laugh, witty beyond his years, and a great guy. Most of the staff had known him for several years longer than I had, but since I was in my mid-twenties and a little younger than most of them, we got along really well.

On this night Ben and I watched a comedy video on and off as I did my rounds and took care of my other patients. I would sit with him when I was charting, and we would catch a laugh. He told me he appreciated the "dude time." He was a trip.

On this unit we took care of adolescents with a variety of illnesses. Sickle cell disease and cancer were the predominant ones. Ben was a bit of an exception as a heart transplant patient, but he always requested to remain on this unit because he had made friends with some of the other kids. It is tough being a teenager even under normal circumstances—much less one with a terminal or chronic disease—so these kids were a great support for each other.

Ben was a little restless that night. I assumed that he was bored. The census was down and his best buddy, Jack, had been discharged earlier that day. I tried to keep Ben entertained but I was a poor substitute for his partner in crime. Around 10 p.m. Ben announced to all within earshot that we were all the most boring people in the world so he was going to sleep. I got him settled, gave him his medications and closed his door. It was even quieter without Ben running around.

At around 2 a.m. Ben emerged, sleepy-eyed, from his room. That wasn't like him. Like most teenagers he would usually sleep through anything. He looked troubled. I asked him if he was all right as he was just standing there in his doorway looking at me. "I'm fine," he said. "I just had the freakiest dream."

"What did you dream about, Ben?" I asked. He told the following story:

> "Well, it was weird because it felt like it really happened. Maybe it was the meds. I dreamt I was downstairs outside and it was

weird because there was no one around. No patients, no doctors or nurses, no cars, nothing. Then I started seeing people appear in the open area in front of the west tower. I started walking towards them and they were, like, glowing or something. They all were standing in a circle holding hands and there was an open spot in the circle and I felt like they were waiting for me.

"I walked over to the spot and I held the hands of the people there. They were all my age. A few were a little younger. To my right there was this really pretty girl with blonde hair and she smiled at me. I didn't know her but I felt like we knew each other or something.

"Then all of a sudden the whole circle took off flying and we landed in my grandfather's yard. I wasn't sure what I should do but no one broke the circle so I just looked at the house. No one talked but I could kind of read their minds like I had some sort of power. They were telling me that they loved me, or I felt like they were. It was like we were all really close, like best friends, but more. Next thing I knew, we took off again and landed at a few other houses and then we came back. I let go of their hands and then—bam—I woke up."

"Wow, Ben, pretty weird," I said. "Did you know any of the people or did any of the places look familiar?"

"No, I only recognized the downstairs area outside and my grandfather's house where I live," he replied. "It just felt so real. When I woke up I wasn't sure if I had really gone downstairs or something."

"No, dude, you were in bed," I reassured him. "Can I get you anything? Are you okay? I was coming in to take your vitals anyway."

"Just some water, please," he said. "And make sure no more glowing people kidnap me. I'm scared of flying."

He chuckled at his own wisecrack and went back into his room. His vitals were stable and he said he felt totally normal. I wished him a good night and promised him I would ensure that air traffic control kept him on the ground. He took a swing at me with his pillow and missed.

At around 3:30 a.m. one of the mothers who was staying in her child's room came from around the corner. They were about seven rooms down and around the corner from where I was sitting outside of Ben's room. She had a water pitcher in her hand.

"Mrs. Gonzalez, can I get something for you?" I asked. Her daughter was not my patient that night, but I knew them well. Giselle was newly diagnosed with leukemia. They had learned that it was very aggressive and the family had really been through a lot that week.

"No, honey. She just woke up and she's thirsty. I can get it."

"It's okay," I protested. "Let me get that for you and I will bring it in."

She relented, handed me the pitcher and went back to her daughter's room. I got some cold water and found my way over to their room. They had a dim light on and her daughter, Giselle, was sitting up in bed with her mom stroking her hand.

"Hey," she said.

"Hey," I replied. "I got your water for you. How are you feeling?"

"I'm feeling okay, I guess. Just a little nauseous from the chemo but I just took my nausea pills."

"Oh, is that what woke you up, Giselle?" I asked as I poured her some water.

"No," her mom interjected. "She had a bad dream."

I felt a little bit of a chill go up my spine. "Really? What did you dream about?" I asked. It sounds weird, but I knew what she was about to say.

Giselle explained:

> "Well, I dreamt that I went downstairs and there were all these kids standing in a circle and there was a lot of moonlight shining on them, like a big full moon, but I didn't see the moon. Anyway, they were, like, waiting for me; at least I felt like they were.
>
> "Suddenly I was in the circle and we were flying around and I think I landed at some apartments, and then we landed in front of my school or something, and then I woke up.
>
> "I guess I have all of the homework I am behind on in my mind so that's probably why we went to my school—I don't know. It felt really cool. I felt, I don't know, happy I guess. It was peaceful like we all loved each other. Sounds weird, I know."

"Hey, Rich, you're spilling the water!" I had been so transfixed by her story that I didn't realize that I was overflowing the cup.

"Oh, I am sorry," I said, noticeably flustered.

"Are you okay, honey?" her mom asked me. "You look pale." In truth, I felt like my head was ringing. It was that feeling you get when something really out of the ordinary happens. I felt like I, myself, was dreaming.

"No, I'm okay," I assured her. "Well, I hope you feel better, Giselle. Do you need anything else?"

"No, I'm going to go back to sleep," she joked. "I'm tired from all of the flying around!"

I just nodded and left the room. I stood in the hallway, trying to make sense of what I had just heard. *Maybe she had overheard Ben talking and her subconscious had flipped on the dream switch?* I pondered. *But the rooms were far away. Plus, Ben and I had talked really quietly and he was mostly inside his room. But what else could have logically occurred here?* I was getting a headache.

My charge nurse, LaVonne, came around the corner.

"Rich, what is wrong with you?" she asked. "You look like you're about to fall out!"

LaVonne and I had a great relationship and I could tell her anything. I proceeded to tell her the whole story. She sat down and smiled.

"My friend, there is no way she could've heard Ben from her room," she said. "No way. This is something else. This is something not of this earth."

I didn't know what to believe. Could two people have the same dream a few hours apart? This was not something that I could wrap my brain around.

The shift came to an end and I drove home in a daze. I remember calling my mom and telling her the story. She told me, "Those kids flew with angels." I laughed. Not that I doubt that there are angels; it just seemed that there had to be a logical explanation.

It was difficult for me to sleep that day. I tossed and turned.

On my drive to work, I was still thinking about Ben's dream. He was sleeping when I left that morning so I had not yet told him about Giselle. I was considering whether I should tell them both. I wasn't sure if they would want to know or if it would freak them out.

But when I walked on the unit, something seemed wrong. The first person I saw was Jeanette, our wonderful nurse's aide. Her head was in her hands as she sat at the desk.

"Hey, Jeanette, what's up?" I asked as I tossed my backpack on the desk.

She looked up at me and there were tears rolling from her eyes. When I asked if she was okay, she just shook her head and started sobbing. I went over to her and hugged her. Just then LaVonne came out of the lounge where I could see my coworkers from the off-going shift still huddled in there. She came over to me and put her hand on my arm.

"Baby, Ben got discharged this morning," she said. "He went home and apparently he had some lunch and went to take a shower. His grandfather heard something hit the wall and found Ben on the floor. He died. We just heard from one of the doctors."

I was shocked. Everyone was shocked. Ben had been doing really well. Apparently, he had no symptoms or chest pain, which I learned from his cardiac surgeon is not uncommon with heart transplant patients. I couldn't believe he was gone, just like that.

LaVonne fixed me with that look that she had that meant "listen closely." "Do you remember what you told me Ben dreamt about?" she asked.

"Yes, I've been thinking about it all day."

"Me too. He knew something was going to happen. Those were angels, Rich."

I just stared at LaVonne. Then it hit me. "How is Giselle doing?" I asked.

"She's fine from what I heard in report," said LaVonne. She paused. "Oh. I hear you," she said. "My goodness, do you think...." Her voice trailed away. She rubbed her arms. "I got a chill. This is too much." LaVonne walked away shaking her head.

The whole unit was shaken hard. We loved Ben. He had grown up with us. His loss was ours and we felt it deeply.

I never told Giselle or her mom about Ben's dream being like hers. I thought it might scare them. She had a good night that night. I was her nurse and I probably fussed over her more than normal because I felt like she and I had been part of something.

Giselle was discharged a few weeks later. I did not hear much about her afterwards. Then, one day, I ran into her doctor, who was a wonderful pediatric oncologist. We made small talk and I asked her about one of her patients that I was caring for. She sighed and looked down. "She reminds me of Giselle," she said.

"Oh, I meant to ask how she's doing," I said.

"Oh, you didn't hear? She died at home with hospice three days ago."

My head swam and I sat down hard. "I...I hadn't heard. I am so sorry."

"Me too, she was a sweet girl," said the doctor sadly as she closed the chart and walked away.

What had just happened? What were those dreams all about? Even to this day, I am not 100 percent sure...but I know something happened. I choose to believe that it was something not explained by logic or science. It was something special.

I believe it was something miraculous.

INSPIRATION DESTINATION: NOTICE THE MIRACULOUS.

SPIRITUAL STRETCH #1: During your time as a nurse, have you experienced something that you can't explain? An amazing recovery? A healing that left the team scratching their heads in disbelief?

If you haven't yet experienced that personally, do you know of someone who has? What was his or her story? Maybe in your life outside of work you have been witness to something "miraculous" or have a family story that has been passed down to you. Where has the miraculous touched your life?

Today, take notice of the miraculous. Maybe you are a spiritual person and believe in a Higher Power. Or maybe you are more aligned with science and believe that mysterious phenomena could be explained scientifically. It really doesn't matter. I am choosing the term "miracle," but you may call it something else. Labels aren't important.

What is important is that you get in touch with that which is bigger than you. Journal about what a "miracle" is to you. If it is a story that you recall, write it down. If it is something that you are hoping for, whether it be for a patient or a friend, journal about it.

Perhaps start off by writing "I define a miracle as..." and then take it from there.

SPIRITUAL STRETCH #2: Journal about the miracle you were part of. Journal about the miracle you heard about. Journal about the miracle that you would like to see happen. It is inspirational to connect to that which is "miraculous."

For me, the story of Ben and Giselle, while very sad in one context because two people died at a very young age, also seemed miraculous because other than having the same dream, they both insisted that they felt a strong feeling of "love" during their experiences.

I don't know if their almost identical dreams were a sign, an otherworldly message of love, or a bizarre coincidence. I just know how it felt for me, and how I have chosen to interpret it.

Another facet to explore: If you do believe in miracles, what are their origins? God? Spirit? The Universe? All of the above? What is your favorite concept of a miracle? What is your favorite movie or book about a miracle? Is it a miracle handed down from a religious perspective such as those of the Bible, Torah, or other belief system's religious scholars or writings? How can you inspire yourself or others by inviting miracles into your experience?

Now, share your thoughts with others. Bring up "miracles" today. If you are on this journey with your team, discuss the subject with them. Ask your patients, coworkers, or employees about their experiences with "miracles." Invite miracles to be a part of your day.

CHAPTER

6

INSPIRATION DESTINATION:
GIVE GRATITUDE TO NURSING AIDES/ASSISTANTS

A "JEANNIE" WE ONLY WISH WE COULD BOTTLE

She never said "no." Sometimes that can be a bad thing, I guess, but with Jeannie it was different.

Jeannie, can you please get my patient some ice?...Jeannie, can you help me move him to the chair?...I know you're busy, Jeannie, but when you have a chance, would you feed her for me so I can take my patient to MRI? All of these questions were lovingly answered with a, "Yes, honey. I will take care of it."

We *prayed* for the days when Jeannie would be there. Her spirit lit up the room. Honestly. None of us took advantage of her kindness.

Well, that is only partially true. There were some who did, at first, abuse her generosity, but the rest of us—blindly loyal to our favorite nurse's aide—did not let such behavior stand. Those who dared to trespass across the line we mentally drew to protect Jeannie were quickly "reformed."

Jeannie was a precious treasure. She had an aura of caring around her. She brought out the best in us all and was beautiful on so many levels.

She would bring in food from her dinner for the poor mother sleeping at her child's bedside. She would share her own homemade cookies with the young resident physician too overwhelmed to remember to eat before going on rounds. She would drive an exhausted parent home at the end of her shift so that he wouldn't have to take the bus.

She did it all without fanfare. All without complaint. All with a loving spirit. She made such a difference.

If you're lucky, there is a person like this in your world. Maybe she is a nurse's aide. Maybe she's a secretary, or an assistant, or an intern. Maybe behind every "great nurse" there is another person who knows how to get things done, what the phone numbers are, and how to find stuff.

Who is this person for you?

INSPIRATION DESTINATION: GIVE GRATITUDE TO NURSING AIDES/ASSISTANTS.

SPIRITUAL STRETCH #1: No matter what you do in nursing, someone is there supporting your work. If you are a nursing executive, you may have an assistant, a staff nurse may have nursing aides, a professor may have a teaching assistant, a researcher may have a data processor.

Take a moment to honor the helpers in your life for their support, beyond the "mandatory" Nurse Week or Executive Assistant Week activities. Those are standard for the most part. *This* needs to be from you.

Choose one of your most helpful assistants and let her know that her support is priceless. You can take her out for a meal or a cup of coffee. You can schedule a meeting with her and surprise her with her favorite snack or a team jersey or movie tickets. You can write her a letter or poem or give her a card. You can frame a picture of her child or pet. If you are someone who likes the personal feeling of talking one-on-one, that would be great too.

The method is not nearly as important as the intent. Your goal is simple. Give your gratitude to someone who supports your work. Be specific and let her know exactly what she does that makes such a difference to you.

Don't just say "thanks." Really go out on a limb and define, describe, and share. Give examples of how she makes a difference. Be specific. Remember that recognized behavior gets repeated. Think of this time as not only an investment in your own inspiration but also in the growth and encouragement of someone who works with you...and in the well-being of all the other people whose lives she touches.

Sharing appreciation with those who make it possible for you to do what you do every day is one way to plant the seeds of inspiration. Appreciation is contagious. There is an effect that goes beyond the "measurable." How can you calculate the impact this conversation or gift may have on the recipient?

SPIRITUAL STRETCH #2: Journal how it feels to give this gift of gratitude. What did you see or hear from the one you shared with? What feels different? Would you do it again? Why or why not? If someone recognized you in this way, how would you want them to do so?

CHAPTER 7

INSPIRATION DESTINATION:
MAKE YOUR WORKPLACE
MORE PEACEFUL

THE SWEET SMELL OF PEACE

David is probably the nurse executive I admire most. (He is also like a brother to me.) There were many times I would venture into his office, under the pretense of discussing something important, but really, it was because the place was "peaceful." I could breathe in there. My thoughts were clearer.

Not my office. No way. My office was chaos. I had notes everywhere along with piles of papers and files. I like to think of myself as "organizationally challenged."

David's office, on the other hand, was like a sanctuary of peace and structure. It had tasteful knick-knacks, warm colors, calming fountains, organized and matching desk ornaments. It even *smelled* soothing, like a spa. You and I both know spa-like fragrances are not normal in a hospital.

Sure, people sometimes teased him about it, but they also asked him to help them organize *their* workspaces. Pretty soon the majority of our offices smelled like "Clean Linen" or "Jasmine" as well.

Clearly, David was an influential guy. What's funny is that, as smart and capable as he was in his work, what we cared most about was gleaning his spa-office knowledge!

David had one of the most stressful jobs in the organization, but he maintained an environment that said "peace." You could gather your thoughts in that office. You could solve problems.

The serenity of his office wasn't just for "looks." For him, this peace was as essential as the oils that he kept in the fragrance dispenser plugged into his wall. This was part of his success. We all learned from him.

And the place smelled a whole lot better, too.

INSPIRATION DESTINATION: MAKE YOUR WORKPLACE MORE PEACEFUL.

SPIRITUAL STRETCH #1: Ask yourself, *Is my personal or shared workspace peaceful?* Is there anything I can do to make it more peaceful? Your workspace may be a busy ER, a clinic, an office, a classroom, a skills lab, an ICU, a nursing unit, or any number of other places. So be creative. What can you do to bring peace to your environment?

Here are some suggestions. Try one of these and see what happens.

- Bring a CD player and some "relaxation" music to play in the lounge or office.

- Dim the lights in your office or bring in a lamp to use instead of the bright overhead fluorescents.

- Bring some natural essential oil sprays or pleasant smelling plug-ins and put them in your lounge or office. (Be sensitive to any peers who have allergies, of course.)

- Practice daily self-care. Spend 10 minutes going outside, or somewhere quiet, and breathe deeply. Slow breath in through your nose...hold for a few seconds... slow breath out through your mouth.

- Take a walk outside. Breathe some fresh air. Look at a tree, or a bird, or a patch of flowers. Just get out and think about something that brings you peace. You might even bring someone with you, preferably someone who is stressed out. If you can get him a little more peaceful, everyone will benefit.

Remember, above all, that inspiration and peace need each other to grow. Any time you can bring peace to your work life, you also make room for inspiration. Try introducing peace in any way that you can. Sometimes just the thought of peace can make a difference.

SPIRITUAL STRETCH #2: The nursing environment can sometimes "breed" manic energy. For contrast, think about a bookstore, a house of worship, or a library. Few people walk into these places yelling or talking loudly or fussing. Yet, most of us have seen our peers and coworkers do such things in our own workplace.

Have you ever been to an outstanding hospice unit? I have always noticed the reverence that is given to that environment. There is a respect for the work that is being done there.

Now that you have brought some peace to your own world, share the wealth with others in your organization. For example:

- Make some herbal tea and bring in a big thermos of it for your team. Or bring in a little basket of herbal teabags and lay them out in the lounge or shared space with a note to your coworkers telling them to feel free to have a cup of "peace."

- Post some inspirational quotes in a shared space like a lounge or conference room.

- If you are a leader, contact a massage therapy school and/or pay a therapist to give your staff/team five-minute massages in a quiet, relaxing environment like a lounge or office. Many licensed massage therapists will be happy to do this very inexpensively, because it is a great way for them to build up their clientele.

- Get permission to bring in someone who does pet therapy...for your staff/team. We all know a happy golden retriever can do wonders for our patients, but what about for us? Pet lovers will get a big kick out of the unconditional love animals provide.

- Does your organization offer yoga classes at lunch, or hold meditation times? If so, participate. If not, write a note to your leader and respectfully and earnestly suggest it. Or if you are that leader, find out if this is something your team or organization would be open to...and if they are, lend your support.

CHAPTER 8

INSPIRATION DESTINATION:
WRITE A THANK-YOU NOTE

A ROSE FROM ROSIE

Rosie rarely spoke, but she always smiled. She was an environmental worker, and went about doing her job with dedication. She was someone you could easily walk past because she was so quiet and unassuming.

As it turned out, though, this gentle woman had a powerful impact on many lives.

A nurse manager was rounding on patients one day when she realized it. When she asked her patients, "Who is someone who does a great job and has made a difference for you during your stay here?" several of them answered, "Rosie the housekeeper. She is wonderful."

The manager was surprised. She rarely heard Rosie say a word. Sure, she did a great job cleaning, but she was so quiet. This merited some research, so the manager began to dig deeper. She spoke to staff and to patients. What she found out astounded her.

Rosie often prayed with the more spiritual patients and brought in inspirational reading materials for those who showed an interest in having them.

In addition, she often made "towel animals" for her patients to cheer them up. (She had learned how to make them from her years working on a cruise ship.) These cute works of art often brought smiles to the patients' faces.

During her breaks (and after getting permission), Rosie would sometimes visit an elderly female patient's room to wash and set her hair. This pleased the patients, who usually felt self-conscious about how their hair looked after so many days in the hospital. Having previously worked in her sister's hair salon, Rosie was thrilled to be able to keep her "skills" up. She would never accept a tip. Not only were the patients delighted, the nurses and their aides were thrilled to have the help.

The manager couldn't believe that she was just now hearing this treasure trove of wonderful information. She sat down and wrote a long and well thought-out thank-you note, which she sent to Rosie's home and also to her director.

A few days later, the manager heard a knock on her open door. Looking up, she saw Rosie. She was clutching the note in her left hand and a small rose wrapped in a napkin in her right hand. Tears were running down her face.

Rosie shared that she had been recently diagnosed with cancer and given a poor prognosis. Her husband had recently died, and her son who was in the military was deployed to the middle east for what would be many months.

She added that there were many days when she would do nothing but cry. She told the manager that she had prayed for a sign that life was not only darkness, as it had felt these last few months. Then, the thank-you note arrived from the hospital.

At first Rosie was afraid to open it. She had received so much bad news lately, and what if this was more of the same? When she finally was able to muster the courage to open the letter she couldn't believe her eyes. Here was the sign she waited for! She told the manager that her director posted a copy in the department and they brought in a cake for her to celebrate the good news. This had uplifted her spirit.

The manager was now crying and the two hugged. Rosie handed the manager the rose and told her she had picked it from her own garden. She told the manager that she had restored her faith. She really meant this. As Rosie walked away, two people were forever changed by the simple act of sending a thank-you note. One was encouraged during a very dark time...and another was inspired to find more reasons to say "thank you" every day.

INSPIRATION DESTINATION: WRITE A THANK-YOU NOTE.

SPIRITUAL STRETCH #1: If you run into a Studer Group coach, speaker, or partner, ask her to tell you a story about a thank-you note. My experience has been that she almost always has one.

These notes are powerful things. They take a feeling or thought of appreciation and turn it into something tangible. You can hold them, read and re-read them, and share them with others.

I keep the notes I have received in a box in my office. They inspire me. When I write one, I picture the person getting it out of his mailbox and shuffling the bills and other mail to the bottom of the pile so he can rip into this source of inspiration contained in a thin paper envelope. In my mind's eye I can see his smile. My heart feels good.

Sometimes you even get a "thank you" for your "thank you." Have you noticed that?

Today, write a thank-you note. If you don't have any cards or notes, buy some or make your own. Think of someone who has made a difference for you. It could be a coworker, a friend, a person who gave you great service in a store or restaurant. Think it through. Write it out as specifically as you can.

Now mail the note. Try to get the recipient's home address, or if that is not possible, send it to her place of work. Be sure to mail it, though; there is just something special about getting a note in your mailbox.

There is so much inspiration in this simple act. Inspiration lives in picking out the card, writing the kind words, and reliving the experience as you do so—not to mention the excitement of wondering if she has received it yet!

I promise this will be one of the most transformational experiences you will have on this journey of inspiration. Make it a habit. Living a life where you focus on gratitude is an inspirational thing.

SPIRITUAL STRETCH #2: Now, make it a practice to be more thankful, in general, as you go about your life. Is "an attitude of gratitude" too much of a cliché?

We hear that expression a lot but the rhyme of the two words helps it cling to our minds. Being on purpose in life, being inspired, being passionate—these qualities cannot exist without a sense of gratitude.

Think about those people you know who look for the worst in others. How do they seem to you? Are they happy? Do you envy their journey or want to be like them? I doubt it.

Such people hide behind their sarcasm and witty put-downs so that no one can see how broken-hearted they are. Isn't that sad? To me, the saddest part of all is that they could transform their lives if only they opened their eyes and really noticed the abundance all around them.

Now, look in the mirror. Do you frequently choose cynicism over gratitude? Ask yourself why. Why is it that we often mock those who see the good in the world? Maybe it is our own fear that we will never be that way. Maybe we were taught to think that way. Maybe our life experience has led us down that road.

The good thing about roads, though, is that *you can almost always turn around and take another road.*

Take the risk of being thankful. Act on this today. If you already do this, expand it. Do it more. Do it better. If this is a new concept to you, start now. Yes, now. Now is a good time.

CHAPTER 9

INSPIRATION DESTINATION:
ASK A PATIENT OR COWORKER FOR HIS OR HER "ONE THING"

WHAT YOU GIVE IS WHAT YOU GET

I remember a pivotal moment in my career. I was working on a unit that treated children with cancer. I was new to the department and was soaking up all the knowledge and insights I could from those around me.

One day, a senior nurse took me aside to check in with me and see how I was doing. In the course of our conversation she said something I never forgot. She told me that every day, when first rounding on or assessing her patients, she would ask them, "If there was one thing that I could do for you today to make you feel a little better, what would that one thing be?"

If I would start practicing this, she promised, it would make my day. I immediately set out to give it a try, and it was incredible. For some patients the "one thing" was to have a big cup of ice. For others it was to call their dad at work. For still others it was to keep the lights dim. Such simple things...but what a difference they made!

Here's what occurred to me during this exercise. Maybe when we lose our inspiration, it's because we have decided that being a nurse is all about "me."

Think about that. Do you find yourself in conversations at the nurses' station about how you can make life better for your patients? Do you have uplifting talks in the office where you speak about how to elevate a peer? Or are you surrounding yourself with folks who sometimes are more focused on their own needs? Could you be one of them, or at risk of becoming one of them?

I know I own that shortcoming! Many times I have been that selfish person. Yes, been there, done that. Got the t-shirt *and* the snow globe!

It makes sense. When you are most inspired and most on-purpose, you are not focused on "you." You are focused on the person you are caring for, leading, or teaching. You are giving...and you are most definitely "getting" in return.

INSPIRATION DESTINATION:
ASK A PATIENT OR COWORKER FOR HIS OR HER "ONE THING."

SPIRITUAL STRETCH #1: Hold up the mirror. What do you see? Are you asking those that you serve, "What can I do for you?" or are you asking, "What can you do for me?"

How do you think others perceive you? Is your mirror so fogged up from speaking about yourself that you can't see those standing behind you who really need your support?

Ask a patient, "If there was one thing that I could do for you today to make you feel a little better, what would that one thing be?" Listen to him closely. He may not understand the question. Ask it again.

Your goal here is simple. Find something that you can do for him to bring him some comfort. You will find in that simple act a surprising sense of inspiration.

Maybe you are no longer in patient care. So adjust this practice to fit your own life. Ask a coworker the "one thing" question.

After you pick her up off of the floor, you might be amazed at her response. More importantly you will amaze her with your kindness. She will see you differently. You will feel that incredible sensation of giving back, of making a difference. There is even the possibility that you will have encouraged her to do the same.

SPIRITUAL STRETCH #2: Now that you've seen firsthand the power of asking the "one thing" question, share the technique with your employees or coworkers. Imagine a whole department looking for ways to help each other or ease their patients' discomfort. The good feelings will spread exponentially, to both "askers" and "askees."

Service is so very powerful. Nurses are all about that. It is who we are. It is, mostly, why we do what we do. Be inspired by the difference you can make by making a difference for someone else.

CHAPTER 10

INSPIRATION DESTINATION:
BE WELCOMING OF SPIRIT

THE FIRST GOOD-BYE

It was the early 1990s. AIDS was taking the lives of many people in America. I was in nursing school and was among those healthcare professionals newly learning how to care for these special patients.

We didn't know much about the disease at that time so our precautions were extreme by today's standards. We were told to gown up from head to toe, including face shields, gloves, and masks. Sometimes this made us feel disconnected from our patients, but at the time, as we learned about this unforgiving disease, it was thought to be a necessity.

I had a patient named Jose. He was in the end stage of AIDS. He was a young man of 27 and had been a nurse in his native Cuba. Jose had been in the hospital for quite some time.

I remember thinking that the handsome, movie star-like young man in the pictures all over his hospital room wall barely resembled the grey and emaciated patient sleeping in that hospital bed. Still, even through the ravages of his disease, one could discern that charming young man through his occasional smiles.

Those smiles were, unfortunately, less frequent as he slipped deeper and deeper into his last days. His mother, an ever-present figure by his bedside, sat vigil over her dying son. She was quiet and reverent. Her English was much better than my Spanish and we managed to communicate to the best of our ability.

She always greeted me with a smile and told me that she appreciated how gentle I was with her son. She added that, if he were able, he would have told me that I would make a very good nurse someday. She was being too gracious; most of the time all I was able to do was feed Jose or clean him up. Still, her kind words encouraged me.

I found her, and still find her, amazing. This woman was losing the person she loved most in this world, yet she took the time to encourage me. And she treated everyone in the same manner. All of the students loved her. She exuded kindness. While the word "saintly" is often overused these days, it suited her well. She moved with a peaceful grace, spoke in a gentle tone, and always had a smile and a gracious "gracias" for all who cared for Jose.

On the third day that I was with him, I noticed a sense of urgency in her expression. I came to her side and put my hand on her shoulder. Without saying a word she reached up and held my hand and began praying in Spanish.

I understood some of what she said, but it was as if the words themselves were completely unimportant. Spirit knows no tongue. I bowed my head and entered silently into her spiritual reverie. She leaned forward and kissed Jose's hand, and then, to my surprise, she turned her head and kissed mine.

At that very moment, Jose opened his eyes for the first time in days, turned to his mother, smiled, and left this world. It happened that quickly. She regarded her son with a look that went beyond sadness and grief. She looked almost regal. She held a dignity that I had not seen in anyone before and have never seen since.

She rose to her feet, touched her son's cheek, tucked his blanket around him, and said, "My prayers are answered. You are at peace." She turned to me with such warmth in her eyes and said, "Thank you, my son." With that she gathered her Bible and purse and quietly left the room.

To this day, when I recall this story, I stand in awe of what I was allowed to be a part of.

Jose was the first patient I ever saw die. That is one of those "first" experiences most nurses can always remember. After his mother left, my nursing instructor helped me clean the body and prepare it for the morgue. I remember crying the whole time.

When I left that day I couldn't stop thinking about the feeling in the room when Jose's mother was praying. What a humbling experience that was! I witnessed the purest kind of love. I was allowed, as unworthy as I am, to offer my support to that kind woman. We are so fortunate as nurses to be a part of something so wondrous and sacred.

INSPIRATION DESTINATION:
BE WELCOMING OF SPIRIT.

SPIRITUAL STRETCH #1: Many of us find peace in spirit. Some of us may have a deep relationship with God, others may have a spiritual knowing, still others may have neither. It is what it is.

Personal beliefs aside, are there times when you can be a part of the peace your patients may find in their spiritual walk? Is there a way that you can feed this need that your patients may have?

Much inspiration and peace lie within the realms of prayer, spiritual reading, reflective silence, and meditation. Being a participant in this, at the request of your patients or their families, also invites inspiration into your own journey. Seek these opportunities and they will be presented to you.

Be open to these experiences when they arise. If you are invited, or when it is appropriate, ask your patient if you may meditate with him or pray with or for him. Perhaps his spirit will be renewed if you simply take a moment to sit quietly with him. Maybe he can find spiritual encouragement by your reading to him from his favorite book or playing his favorite music.

Let your patient be your guide. It is an amazing thing to be a part of the full healing process that is body, mind, and spirit. You are serving in a way that cannot be learned but must be experienced.

If you are not providing patient care, perhaps you know someone at work who shares a similar faith or indicates that she follows a praying or meditating path. She may be open to having you pray or meditate with her.

This is a powerful way to "bond" with a coworker and may even lead to a more peaceful work environment. This connection may simply be an opportunity to learn more about what brings peace and comfort to those with whom you spend so much of your time every day.

Do these ideas sound radical to you? That's okay. Maybe being a spiritual rebel will bring you some inspiration.

SPIRITUAL STRETCH #2: Is there a way you can deliberately—while maintaining respect for those who don't share your beliefs—infuse your environment with spirituality? I know, I know. People get all weird when you talk about religion. (It's right up there with politics!) But think about this: Numerous polls show that the majority of people, in the United States for example, believe in God or some Higher Power. Therefore the majority of people you come in contact with are most likely familiar with some form of spirituality. However, one needs to be respectful of those who do not share these kinds of beliefs.

It cannot be argued that some people are comforted through a spiritual connection. Put your feelings aside for a moment and ask yourself if you can help your patients and/or coworkers find spiritual solace.

Maybe spirituality is just not you. Maybe you do not consider yourself "spiritual" in any way. No harm, no foul. If your patient has a need for a spiritual boost, maybe you can simply offer to wheel him down to the chapel on your break, or buy him a book he indicated he might like, or arrange to have members of his place of worship gather with him. If you don't feel like you can be a participant, can you find ways to be an agent?

Outside of the patient care setting you may offer to lead prayer or meditation sessions, or incorporate connect-to-purpose moments into your meetings for peers or coworkers. These moments can consist of inspirational quotes, encouraging stories, or uplifting letters from patients. Be open to the idea of bringing comfort of spirit, regardless of what that looks like. The "label" is not as important as the purpose.

How can you make spirit a part of your inspired journey?

CHAPTER

11

INSPIRATION DESTINATION:
INCREASE AND IMPROVE
PATIENT SAFETY

THE FOUR FAVORS

His name was Kevin and he was fourteen years old. I had been taking care of him for a few months in the intensive care unit. He had a rare auto-immune disorder and had been on a long road toward recovery. As I cared for him, we bonded.

I don't know what it was—most nurses I worked with tended to gravitate toward the "cute" babies and toddlers—but Kevin and I just took to each other. I saw something special in him. In fact, he was like a little brother to me.

Kevin was still a patient when Christmas came around. Every year, a kind person would donate toys to the unit to be given out to the kids who would "celebrate" their holiday in an intensive care unit. This particular year we received a donation of teddy bears.

Don't get me wrong, they were cute bears...but how much do you think the typical fourteen-year-old boy wants a teddy bear? Not so much.

Inspired Nurse

65

Still, I had an idea. Digging through the pile of bears, I found it! The one! It was a motorcycle bear.

I approached Kevin with the bear behind my back and a goofy look on my face. I presented it to him with much fanfare.

Not surprisingly, Kevin turned red (it doesn't take much to embarrass a teenager). He got the joke and shook his head. He pretended to "love" his stuffed animal and proceeded to throw it at every doctor and nurse who walked by. We had a rare moment of levity and it was good.

Kevin got a little better and we were gearing up for his discharge home. I wasn't going to be there over the weekend that he would be discharged. I spent a few minutes with him and his mom, to whom I had grown close, saying my good-byes as I ended my shift.

He had already begun packing his things even though discharge was at least two days away. I noticed that one thing had not yet been packed. Winking at his mom, I grabbed the bear and approached Kevin in mock seriousness. "Mr. Bear is very sad that you forgot him, Kevin." I said in a childlike voice. "Whatever, dude," he replied.

He smacked the bear out of my hands and tossed it at my head. We laughed and I gave him and his mom a high-five good-bye. As I walked out of the room, out of the corner of my eye, I saw him pick the bear up and toss it into his bag.

Busted! I smiled, said a silent prayer for him, and went on my way.

A few weeks after Kevin's discharge, I came in for what I thought would be a "normal" shift. As I came to the unit door, I saw a familiar face standing there. It was Kevin's mom. She looked calm, so I assumed that Kevin had been readmitted for some observation or IV treatments.

When she saw me, she made a beeline for me. "Hey, Rich, I was waiting for you. Obviously, Kevin is back. We aren't sure what happened, but I wanted to ask you a favor."

"Sure," I said. "What can I do?"

She fixed her eyes to mine and said, "I want you to be Kevin's nurse tonight."

"Absolutely, we can do that," I said. Something felt different to me. She had an intensity about her that was not usual. "Is everything okay?" I asked.

"No," she said. "I know that Kevin is going to die tonight and I want you to be his nurse."

I almost fell to the ground. This was not what I expected. I hugged her and reassured her that I would be there for them both.

After I got the report, I understood that Kevin was in grave condition. The team did all that they could. I was standing on Kevin's left side holding his hand. His mom was on his right. There were no more medications that we could give. This brave young man who had fought for so long and so valiantly was ready to end his battle.

His heart slowed. *110, 80, 70, 55, 40, 20.* Peace. His mom leaned over and kissed her beautiful son on the forehead and my "little brother" died. It wouldn't be until much later that we would learn that it was a post-discharge medication error that led to Kevin's death.

Standing there at the bedside, his mom looked up at me. "Rich, I have another favor to ask you."

"Anything you need, Mom," I said as we both wiped away tears.

"I've already planned Kevin's funeral and it would mean a lot to me if you would go."

I had never been to a patient's funeral before but this was different. "Sure," I said. "I will be there for you."

Touching my hand, she said, simply, "You always were."

I dreaded the day. I found my way to the funeral home. There were hundreds of people there, it seemed. Most of them were Kevin's friends. There were other doctors and nurses there who had cared for Kevin. He meant a lot to us. The team had worked hard for him. They cared about him. This loss was devastating to us all.

My memory of the day is foggy. As many times as I tell the story, it seems that I have to push myself to recall certain details. Yet other details are crystal clear. Isn't that interesting how the mind works? Still, I remember the next part very well.

I tried to lose myself in the crowd. Kevin's mom found me, though, and gave me a big hug. "I am so glad you are here," she said.

I smiled weakly, feeling like I wanted to crumble at this woman's feet. I knew how broken my heart was, and I couldn't imagine how she felt. "Rich, can I ask you another favor?" I nodded. "Would you please come up to see Kevin with me?"

This was what I feared. On the drive there I told my wife that as long as I didn't have to see him in the coffin, I could keep it together. A few years before at my own father's funeral, my two wonderful big brothers had practically dragged me over to see my dad. (They knew from experience that it would offer closure for me, and they were right, as big brothers usually are.)

What could I say? I had to do this. "Okay, Mom," I said.

She took my arm and began leading me toward Kevin. All eyes were on us. People parted before us as we walked, for what seemed to be miles, towards that coffin.

There he was. She hugged me. Shouldn't it be me comforting her?

"What do you think?" she asked.

What was she asking me? My mind raced, and I said what everyone says when standing at the side of a coffin. "He looks peaceful," I replied, lamely.

She smiled. "No, Rich, look closer."

I did. I noticed that his sports team had signed a jersey and it was with him in the coffin. "Oh, his jersey. That is wonderful. He would have liked that."

"No, Rich, look closer."

My eyes were so full of tears I had not noticed a very important detail. In the coffin, next to Kevin, was the teddy bear that I had given him. The very one we threw at each other that last Christmas. The one I saw my buddy put in his backpack when he thought no one else was looking. It was with him.

Then his mom turned me around to look at her. "Rich, I have one more favor to ask you. You're a young guy and you have your whole life ahead of you and I hope a long career. You and the nurses and doctors who cared for Kevin made a huge difference in our lives. Kevin loved you. He always asked if you were working, and when he knew you were going to be there, I could tell he felt at ease. So did I. So I have a favor to ask.

"Rich, Kevin is gone," she continued. "I will never hear his voice, touch his hand, or see his smile again. That is a reality. But I want him to live on in some way. I want you to promise me that you will never forget him. I want you to keep a part of Kevin with you every time you care for a patient or comfort a family. If you can promise me that then I will know that he will continue to live on. Can you do that for me?"

I was stunned. Who was I to be asked this honor? It was an easy promise to make. I would never forget this boy. "I promise I will," I said while both of us dried the copious tears that wouldn't end. We hugged and with one last glance at that precious young man's face, I left her standing there gazing lovingly at the son who would live on only in the thoughts and memories of those of us so privileged to have had him in our world.

I was changed forever.

When we learned about the medication error later on, it was as if he had died all over again. His physicians were crushed. The nurses were brokenhearted. While certainly it was Kevin and his family who took the full force of this, we, his caregivers, were the second victims of this unfortunate error.

Later on, I would become a risk manager and patient safety director. Much later on I would become a coach with Studer Group and have the opportunity to speak about the amazing work that Studer Group does to impact patient safety.

I share Kevin's story everywhere I go. It still brings me to tears, although I have told the story a hundred times. As I write this down, for the first time in a decade, I have to stop and walk around to shake it off so that I can get through the story. I still feel its impact.

Recently, I ran into one of the wonderful physicians who cared for Kevin at one of my presentations. She had been at the funeral those many years ago. She told me that she thinks of Kevin almost daily and that his memory reminds her that we have a sacred task to protect our patients. They depend upon us.

When we fail to keep them safe, we certainly hurt our patients and their families, but we also rob ourselves. I feel that we cannot be inspired or inspirational unless we recognize our sacred duty to protect our patients from harm.

INSPIRATION DESTINATION: INCREASE AND IMPROVE PATIENT SAFETY.

SPIRITUAL STRETCH #1: I have had the honor of speaking about patient safety to thousands of healthcare providers all around the country. It always touches and humbles me when people take the time to approach me after I have spoken and share stories about either their professional or personal experiences with this issue. It inspires me every time.

What I have learned from these wonderful people is that not only is inspiration drained from us when we learn of (or worse, are a part of) a medical error, but also that it's gained when we know we have protected our patients and ensured that their care was safe.

So what can you do to increase and improve patient safety? If you are a teacher, you can ask your students to share what they have learned about patient safety, or come up with questions that they may have to discuss with the group. Or they can share observations they have made during clinical rotations of examples of safe or unsafe care. By doing this, you plant a seed for your students.

If you are a leader, how about scheduling daily patient safety huddles with your team? You can even use some of the above examples given for instructors and instead relate them to employees. How about rounding on your staff and asking them if they have any ideas to improve patient safety? Ask them if they have learned any best practices, what they think could be done better in regard to patient safety, and what is already done well.

Studer Group has an amazing Patient Safety Toolkit that has many practical suggestions for ways that individuals and organizations can improve patient safety. There are many resources out there. Look for them.

If you provide direct patient care, what can you do to improve patient safety? Why not review fall precautions with one of your at-risk patients? Ensure that your patients have everything within reach so that they don't fall out of bed reaching for a phone or the garbage pail. Let each patient know that you will frequently ask her to repeat her name or that you will be checking her armband to ensure that you safely provide medication.

Encourage your patients to ask questions or alert you or others if they are concerned with a medication or treatment. Finally, inform your patients that you will wash or cleanse your hands before and after contact with them and that you want them to remind you and others if that doesn't happen.

These are some ways that you can find inspiration in the work that you do. Be creative. Come up with your own ways that you can make this part of your journey to inspiration.

Your work is sacred. Your patients and your team depend upon you. The rewards here are great.

SPIRITUAL STRETCH #2: When I speak to hospital organizations about patient safety, I often share that we are the "second victims" when errors occur. Each of us in healthcare carry the burden of errors committed, either by us personally or by our team or organization. I shared one of mine in an earlier chapter. It is still vivid for me.

Choose to not dwell on each error you have made, but rather on how you can prevent it from happening again. Maybe you can get a like-minded group together, and the group can take a "safety pledge" where you promise to support each other in various measures to improve patient safety like hand washing, medication administration, or training, for example.

This is only one idea. There are infinite others. What comes up for you? How can you learn and grow from your mistakes?

CHAPTER
12

INSPIRATION DESTINATION:
SEEK THE GOOD IN OTHERS

THE OUTSIDER

"She's a snob," said my coworker. "She thinks that she is above everyone."

My coworker was speaking about Elaine, the "new" nurse. Now, Elaine had been a nurse for around fifteen years and had worked in some pretty impressive organizations in the Northeast, but as far as some members of the group were concerned, she was new.

Elaine kept to herself, initially. It's not that she was rude; she was simply very reserved and, honestly, some folks weren't exactly rolling out the welcome mat. Plus, she earned some unfair disdain when, in a staff meeting during her second week, she pointed out a practice that she observed that was less than safe. Never mind that she was correct; some folks just didn't appreciate being schooled by the "new kid."

Two members of the team, who for some reason felt a little threatened by Elaine, started to run their campaign against her. One charge nurse, in particular, went out of her way to tell the others that she was going to go over Elaine's notes with a fine-toothed comb and "bust her" on something just to keep her humble.

In short, it looked like things were going to get ugly. And that's when Shannon—one of the most senior nurses on the unit and the undisputed best nurse there, in many of our minds—stepped up to the plate. What she did was incredible.

One night when Elaine was off but the majority of the "trouble makers" were working, Shannon gathered us together for a meeting. She had made multiple copies of something and handed them out. She asked us to read these first before anyone spoke.

It turned out to be a list detailing Elaine's background and experience. We were amazed to find that she was an army nurse and had won awards for heroism in the field. She was an orphan who, while raised in foster homes, managed to remain on an honors list and get a full scholarship to nursing school.

For the last ten years, she had worked at least one overtime shift per month for the sole purpose of donating that money to programs that help foster children get school supplies. Elaine had won numerous awards for charity, teaching, and clinical expertise.

The second page was even more remarkable. Shannon had listed the name of almost everyone who worked in the department. Next to the names was a sentence or two.

The group was stunned. Obviously, Shannon had been spending a little time with Elaine getting to know her, but she had taken it a step further. She had asked Elaine to observe us and then to share one positive impression about each of us. She then asked each of us to read, aloud, what Elaine had to say about us. The two nurses who were Elaine's most verbal critics actually choked up reading theirs.

Shannon ended the meeting by pointing out that we had not given Elaine a chance and that we had gone out of our way to make her feel uncomfortable. She added that since Elaine so easily determined the good in each of us, didn't we owe her the same?

The people who saw the good in Elaine felt vindicated. The others, while maybe a bit ashamed, saw the error of their ways. Things changed.

It is amazing to look back on that night and the lessons we learned. It is also worth noting that a few months later, Elaine was one of the leaders of the group. She regularly took the lead in presenting new information, organized mission trips to help patients in faraway places, created programs for the patients and the staff, and became a very good friend to all of us.

She remained there for a number of years until accepting a leadership position in another organization. She is as well thought of there as she ended up being in the department that initially didn't see the good in her.

I ran into Elaine not too long ago. She shared with me that any time she hires a new employee, he is first "peer interviewed" so that the staff has buy-in upfront. She gets a great biography on him, which she shares with the rest of the department. She also asks the new employee to make a few observations for her. He must name at least one positive thing he notices about his coworkers over a four-week period. Then, Elaine shares these with the team.

Wonder how she thought of that?

It is truly amazing what you see when you look for the good in others.

INSPIRATION DESTINATION:
SEEK THE GOOD IN OTHERS.

SPIRITUAL STRETCH #1: Your challenge is simple: Look for something good in each person you encounter today, whether they're coworkers, friends, employees, or simply strangers you pass in the hallway.

This exercise will challenge you more than you expect—especially if you encounter someone with whom you have clashed in the past or simply "don't like." Challenging yourself in this way affords you the opportunity to improve your work life. Really.

My hope is that you will recognize that we each *decide* that someone is "bad" or "stupid" or "fun" or "wonderful." If you can find the good in others for just one day (as a start) how can you expand it? Start looking for opportunities to be encouraged and impressed and inspired. You will find that this opens your heart for more inspiration.

SPIRITUAL STRETCH #2: If you are taking this journey with someone else, share what it was like to spend a day looking for the good. If you want to make it more "public," tell someone about the good you observed in her. Who knows? You may encourage someone who was feeling down, you may make a new friend, or you may create peace between you and someone you have not gotten along with in the past.

CHAPTER 13

INSPIRATION DESTINATION:
LOOK FOR REASONS TO BE INSPIRED

THE GIFT

I believe that inspiration can be found wherever we look for it, but "looking for it" are the operative words. At first glance, that might sound a bit "mystical," but I believe it is true. What we put our mind and attention to somehow manifests in our reality. If you focus your thoughts, prayers, meditations, and conversations toward inspiration, then inspiration will find you.

I remember the family who, for me, illustrates this principle. When I close my eyes, I can see them clearly. Their story is tragic. Beyond tragic. Yet the way they handled their circumstances was simply miraculous.

Their thirteen-year-old daughter, Marianne, was playing in a hot tub with her siblings and cousins. When they got out to grab lunch, she said she would follow in a minute. Here's what her family assumes happened next: She leaned back to submerge her long, beautiful hair so that she could get it out of her face. As she did so, her hair caught in the bottom drain of the hot tub. Somehow, the drain cover was off, and Marianne was pulled to the bottom. No one could see her because of the bubbling water. By the time her family noticed she was missing and came upon her in the tub, she was barely clinging to life.

I was Marianne's nurse. It was hard to not get a lump in my throat every time her mom or dad would come to her bedside and talk to her. The whole team felt that way. We were helpless. You could feel their love for her and each other. Her dad had been told that she was brain dead and that nothing could be done for her.

The physician and I approached her dad and discussed allowing her to be an organ donor. These are never easy conversations to have. These days organ donation conversations are often initiated by those who specialize in this area, but back then many of us were trained do so. The father asked if he could go get her mother before we talked further.

Then when it was the four of us, he held her hand and said to his wife, "We will never know the reason that this happened. We are in what feels like a bad dream and there is nothing but darkness around us. Now there is a chance for there to be some light. Honey, remember that couple we've been talking to in the waiting room who are waiting for a liver for their son, and if he doesn't get it he will die this week?"

His wife nodded, looking quietly into his eyes.

"Marianne can live on forever in that boy," he continued. "Just a few minutes ago you and I were talking about asking the docs if she could be an organ donor and now here they are...surely it was meant to be."

The mom dropped her gaze from her husband to her daughter. I can only imagine what she was thinking. After a minute of contemplation she hugged her husband and through her tears said, "This was what I was praying would happen. I needed some good. Something to cling to that would do honor to her life. She was all about helping others; this is what she would've wanted."

I was in awe. I have rarely witnessed such grace and kindness in the midst of such pain and sorrow. It was amazing. During the most tragic moment of their lives, they looked for beauty. They were open to life in the face of death. They were open to giving someone else a miracle even though there would be no miracle for their own loved one.

I was with them when they said good-bye to their daughter as she was wheeled into the operating room where she would make the ultimate sacrifice so that others might live. It was a moment, not marked by words but by the deepest love that you can imagine. They were a beautiful family.

While it wasn't "officially" disclosed to them, they and the other family knew that Marianne was to live on in that young man. Families often get close in waiting rooms as they share stories, food, and hugs. They figured out pretty quickly when each overheard and watched each other have discussions with various teams that Marianne was to be the giver of life for the little boy.

After the family said their good-byes to Marianne, I said good-bye to them. The father's simple "Thank you" to the staff was the most heartfelt two words I had ever heard uttered by a human being. As they walked out, I realized that I had been in the presence of something sacred. Something inspiring.

As fate would have it, I was the little boy's nurse on the day of his surgery. It went well. The gifted surgeons, nurses, Intensive Care Unit physicians, and respiratory team did amazing work.

The boy's parents were grateful for the second chance their son was receiving. They shared with me that they only left the hospital for a few hours during those weeks and it was to attend Marianne's funeral. They had her school picture in a frame at their son's bedside. The mom often said that she felt like Marianne was an angel looking over them. I didn't doubt that for a second.

A few days after his surgery, I was caring for him again when a coworker asked if he could have visitors. "Of course," I said. I had my back to the door, and as I heard someone approach I looked up. There were the boy's parents and two other people. It was Marianne's mom and dad.

Wordlessly, they hugged me. I was speechless, too. They had just buried their beautiful daughter days before. They each knelt on a side of the bed and touched the boy's hands. The unit became absolutely still as everyone realized the gravity of the occasion. I walked away from the bed to give them some privacy and stood quietly with some of the other nurses and doctors at a respectful distance.

Marianne's mom stood up and kissed the boy on the forehead, her tears falling onto his face. As she wiped her tears from his skin, she spoke to this boy to whom her daughter had given new life. "I love you," she said, in the way that only a mother can.

Marianne's dad smiled at this boy as if he were his own child. In many ways, he was. They hugged the boy's parents and slowly made their way out of the unit.

It was one of those moments where time seemed to stand still. The moment encapsulated the beauty of giving, the blessing of sacrifice and the best example of love that I have ever had the privilege of witnessing.

INSPIRATION DESTINATION:
LOOK FOR REASONS TO BE INSPIRED.

SPIRITUAL STRETCH #1: You have one goal today. Be "present" in all that you do. Listen for words that inspire you. Look for deeds that inspire you. Prepare yourself to hear stories that will inspire you.

It is a funny truth that when you look for something, or introduce something into your awareness, it suddenly becomes evident everywhere.

This happens sometimes with names. Let's say you hear an unusual name like Wynter. The next day you have a food server named Wynter. Then, a week later, you hear a parent in the grocery store address her child as Wynter. It's not that there are suddenly more people in the world named Wynter; it's merely that you have become aware of that name.

What if you challenged yourself to become aware of inspiration? What if this became a habit? You often see the opposite. People look for reasons to be insulted or outraged and they are never disappointed, are they? Why not do the opposite? Why not look for reasons to be inspired instead?

This takes a bit of preparation. On your way into work or for the first few minutes before you walk in the door, take a time-out. Quietly say to yourself *I am going to hear inspiration, see inspiration, and feel inspiration everywhere I turn today. I am open to it...bring on the inspiration.*

It will be an incredible experience, if you are truly open to it. Now don't expect to levitate or anything, but notice how differently things appear to you. Be on an all-out hunt for inspiration.

Do you see someone who, despite a challenge, whether physical, emotional, or situational, is overcoming the hurdle and succeeding? That's inspirational. Do you work with someone who maintains an unbelievably positive attitude? That's inspirational. Do you see a family offer each other comfort at the bedside of their loved one, or encounter a peer who is making strides with a student, or witness some great news shared? That's inspirational.

That which dwells in your consciousness, be it unhealthy or nurturing, is what manifests in your life. Inspiration is literally all around you. Invite it in. Give it life within you.

SPIRITUAL STRETCH #2: What did you learn today? Ponder the lesson. Was the inspiration you encountered something new...or something that you simply did not see before? Can you do this on subsequent days? What if you tried it at home?

Now, spend a day looking for inspiration in your world outside of work. How could you see your child, wife, husband, friend, significant other, or parents as inspirational beings?

This is where your journal comes in handy. Write these experiences down. They become tangible for you when you can revisit them. It is awe-inspiring when you become aware of all of the inspiration in your world.

CHAPTER

14

INSPIRATION DESTINATION:

SHARE YOUR STORIES

FUN AT THIRTY-FIVE THOUSAND FEET

I was going on vacation with my beautiful wife Dawn, who also happens to be one of the best nurses I know. At the time she was an amazing E.D. and Trauma nurse; now she is a nursing professor who brings new inspired nurses into the field. They are blessed to have her, as am I.

We were both excited to get away and have some fun. An hour into our flight, the flight attendant got on the microphone and asked if there were any physicians on board. We both stopped our conversation and I know we had the same thought. *Uh-oh.*

A few seconds later the flight attendant asked if there were any nurses present. We both raised our hands.

It turned out that a passenger was apparently reacting to anesthesia from the surgery he had undergone a few hours before. It was probably not a good idea for him to be flying but, nonetheless, here he was.

The flight crew seemed thankful that there were two nurses on board. They looked a little afraid of the medical equipment they brought to us, but, bless them, they were ready to do whatever we needed.

Luckily, there was no need for heroics. The patient was fairly stable. And even more luckily, my wife took over and knew exactly what to do. She was awesome. I, on the other hand, did do a very good job of handing things to her.

Our patient was better, and he, his wife, and the crew were extremely appreciative. My wife, once again, made me look good. Passengers applauded and several offers to buy us drinks rolled in from many passengers. I don't drink, so I passed on the offer. Dawn said, "I'll have his, too." Hey, she did all of the work anyway.

Within a few minutes my wife and I started sharing nursing stories. Many forgotten memories came to our minds. I made her cry and she made me laugh so hard I almost had a nosebleed. It was one of the best conversations that we had ever had.

Our long flight went by in a flash. As we were landing she said, "Don't we nurses have the best stories? No matter what a nurse does or where we've worked, it is a bond we all share."

My wonderful wife really got me thinking. There is great power in our stories. I felt inspired by her stories and by the retelling of my own. That flight was truly an "elevating" experience!

INSPIRATION DESTINATION: SHARE YOUR STORIES.

SPIRITUAL STRETCH #1: Storytelling goes back to ancient times. Stories about great battles, storms, events, and people help us know who we are and where we came from. They were etched on cave walls, written on papyrus, carved in stone, and passed down through the generations in tales told at countless firesides under an eternity of stars. Stories are our history. They tell of the founding of a great nation, the defeat of tyrants, and the birth of freedom.

There are great stories in healthcare. In Studer Group we often say that great organizations are known by the stories that they tell. How true that is! Think about your stories. I have started many of these Inspiration Destinations with a story from my journey. While some names and details have been changed to respect privacy, they are true stories that have brought me through my nursing journey. Regardless of your specialty or where you worked, no doubt we could sit down and share our stories for hours.

We could cry together and recall the great loss and pain that we have witnessed during our respective healthcare journeys. We could also laugh until our stomachs ached at some of the ridiculous things that we have seen and heard.

This destination is about your story.

What is the toughest thing you can ever recall having dealt with during your healthcare journey? Was it a person? A natural or man-made disaster? How did it change you? How did it change your life perspective? Did you almost throw in the professional towel?

Now what's the funniest thing that has ever happened to you? The most absurd situation you have ever been in? It's okay if it is a little "out there." It's good to laugh.

If you are fortunate enough to be on this inspiration journey with another nurse or some of your team, share your stories with each other. Make some time to do this. It is very inspiring. If you are on this journey, it can still be fun to share a story with a colleague. Who knows, perhaps your stories will inspire others to join you.

The thing is, the nurse you are now was created by those stories. They molded you. They are your history. There is much inspiration in your most powerful moments. Share them. Recall them. Carve them into the (metaphorical) cave wall. They will be inspiring to you and those you share them with.

SPIRITUAL STRETCH #2: I knew a nurse who went to school with me and started a journal during her first year of school. Last I heard she was still journaling. She shared with an acquaintance that she has dozens of diaries and they contain all of the key moments of her nursing career. I wish I had done that.

Your journal is crying out to you right now. Write your stories down. Take your time. Throw yourself into it, or if you're inclined, video yourself telling your stories. Then read/watch your storytelling. Cry. Laugh. Remember.

Think about the stories your parents told you. If you were fortunate enough to have had a relationship with grandparents or even great-grandparents, do you remember the stories they would tell? Our history allows us to reflect, refresh, and learn. Our stories make our experiences tangible. Stories allow us to hold our reality in our hands. Tell your stories.

CHAPTER

INSPIRATION DESTINATION:
APPRECIATE HUMOR

WHY DOES EVERYTHING HAPPEN
ON TACO SALAD DAY?

They were unusual times. The Anthrax scare was in full swing. Every
letter and package was being scrutinized carefully. We didn't know who
was sending these letters at the time and when another one would show
up. We were concerned that hospitals could be future targets. Our staff
were all trained in how to respond. We would get through this.

I was the manager of a busy E.D. and it was packed to the rafters. Each
wall had a stretcher. We were jamming. It was a busy day, but a good
one. We were fully staffed, I had a great team on, and today was taco
salad day in the cafeteria—you know, the great meal they served you in
these cool taco shell bowls. Life was good.

Now, just to set the stage, I was at my desk working on the schedule. My
staff did "self-scheduling." You know how that can be. I called it "guided
self-scheduling." I was trying to do the same complicated mathematical
equation that all nurse managers struggle with: If a schedule has four

Fridays and 100 staff members and zero staff members sign up for the Fridays, how many nurse managers have to reach for their antacid? You know the drill. Luckily, for me, we always worked it out.

Anyway, I was focused intently on the schedule when my focus was interrupted by a familiar voice. It was Johnny, our security officer. He's a great guy who would do anything for us.

"Uh, Rich, I think we have a major problem," said Johnny. He put a large box on my desk. I think it was so close to me that it actually brushed my nose when he put it down.

"Okay, Johnny, what's up?" I said, eyeing the box suspiciously.

I noticed that Johnny had not removed his hand from the box and that either the box was vibrating or Johnny's hand was shaking. Johnny said, "Rich, I think this is a bomb."

Okay, so here's where my mind began to really multi-task. Here were my thoughts, as I recall them, in no particular order:

1. Why does Johnny want to kill me?
2. Please, God, let it be his hand that is shaking and let it not be that the box is vibrating.
3. Please, God, make his hand stop shaking.
4. If the bomb goes off, will I still have to staff those Fridays?
5. This can't be real.
6. What if this is real?
7. Why did this have to happen on taco salad day?
8. What do I do?

9. I'm the chairperson of the disaster team—I'm supposed to know.
10. If this is real, people may die.

Now, all of these thoughts flashed through my mind in the space of about two seconds. I would love to tell you that I then said something that exuded leadership and valor but I don't think I did. I am pretty sure the next words out of my mouth were, "Why did you bring the bomb into my office, Johnny?"

He just looked at me. "I guess to get it out of triage," he said. Now that might sound really impressive to you, except that to get it from triage into my office there was only one path. That path was through two doors, through the main E.D. patient area, where all the patients and staff happened to be, past the trauma room, and into my office.

The blood drained from both of our faces. Especially my face, which was still two inches from the box. I stood slowly, eyeing the box with disbelief and growing dread. On the top of the box was writing. It read: "God be with the ER."

In a different time and place that might sound nice. In this situation you can understand if we may have construed it to have a not-so-nice meaning. I had to think. Johnny's hand was still on the box and it was sweating. Was sweat good for a bomb? What if this was a "sweat-triggered bomb"? Was there such a thing? I wasn't sure.

Then the nurse in me kicked in. My racing mind slowed itself down. I could do this. "Johnny," I said, "we have to alert the authorities, close down this area, evacuate the E.D., and protect our patients." I was back in the game.

"I shouldn't have brought this in here," said Johnny. "I don't know what I was thinking."

Before I could reassure him—and much to my horror—Johnny picked up the box, with his sweaty, shaking hands, and ran from my office toward the ambulance doors and into the outside world.

I swear to you at that very second someone in the E.D. dropped a backboard, which made a huge crash when it struck the ground. I threw myself to the floor. For some reason seeing the manager hit the ground attracted a lot of attention from my staff. Just as a sidebar, it's hard to look like you're "in charge" in a fetal position.

By this time other security folks showed up and I had them call the police and alert Administration. When Administration heard that there was a "possible bomb on the campus," they did exactly what they were supposed to do. They called me.

My pager had rolled under a trauma stretcher when I took the appropriate defensive bomb protecting position. (Okay, from when I fell to the ground.) Someone grabbed it and said, "Rich, Administration is paging you 911!"

One of my staff called them back. "Rich, they want you to know that there is a bomb on campus and for you to take the lead, activate the team, and let them know what the next steps are." All-righty then. But, where was Johnny?

I ran out the door with security guards close behind. To my left I could see Johnny and his box. He made his way to the large pond that is in the front of the campus and had placed the box between the pond and a parking lot. The physicians' parking lot, to be specific.

Johnny was now running toward us. "I'm sorry, Rich. I just wanted to get the bomb away from the patients."

Of course when we reviewed all of this later, there were a million things that went wrong. We learned from those, but in Johnny's mind, as he was running with the box that may have contained a bomb, he was trying to save lives.

At this point the authorities began to arrive and the story began to come together about the box.

Apparently a man had approached the triage nurse, Dina. He walked in with the box and said in what Dina perceived to be a "threatening" way, "This is for the E.D." He then "ran" out the door. Johnny was nearby so she called him over. He read the top of the box, heard the fear in Dina's voice, and made the split-second decision to get the box out of triage... and into my office...and now apparently alongside some very nice cars belonging to our medical staff.

The authorities were now taking over. One cop asked me if I was hurt in the scuffle with the guy who delivered the box. I looked at him like he was crazy. He pointed to my elbow, which was bleeding. Before I could speak, my secretary who witnessed my reaction to the backboard dropping told him, "No, he got scared when someone dropped something and he fell."

"Oh," said the cop.

I asked him not to put that in the report. He said he had to.

A lot happened very quickly. The area was taped off, and the road into the hospital was closed. There were dozens of police cars and firetrucks everywhere, and the doctors' parking lot was sealed off. No one could get in or out of the lot.

One of the cops asked Johnny why he put the box so close to the parking lot and Johnny told them that he figured the water on one side offered a natural barrier to the street and the cars in the parking lot would protect the building. (This made Johnny really popular with the doctors when that got out!)

Now this was getting serious. It seemed as if each time Dina was interviewed the story got a little more intense. I think it got to the point that she said that after the guy put the package on her desk and ran out she heard him give an evil laugh. Dina definitely had a dramatic flair.

The bomb squad was there. They evacuated a nearby building. It happened to be a doctors' office. They were all standing behind us. They had nowhere to go anyway because their cars were all blocked off.

The bomb squad folks were nice enough to put a large, thick tarp over some of the nearby cars in the physicians' parking lot, which then set one of the car alarms off. As if we needed more drama, one of the firefighters began rushing toward the alarming Audi with his ax because the bomb guys were afraid the alarm would set off the "bomb." One of the docs standing behind us lifted his key and shut the alarm off. The firefighter looked disappointed.

Now, they had us at a safe distance. They had somehow determined that there were no biohazards in the box. A bomb squad member in a huge bomb suit placed some stuff near the box and we were told that they were going to blow it up. At this point there were several news trucks there also. We heard the countdown and then there was a muted pop.

When my eyes opened, it looked like it was snowing. I was standing next to the hospital Chief Operating Officer and she and I both noticed that little squares of something were landing on our heads. I removed one and looked at it. It was a little piece of cloth with a bunny picture on it.

She removed a piece that landed in her hair. Hers was a piece of cloth with a famous mouse and his mouse wife.

That's right. This appeared to be a bomb loaded with cute pictures drawn on cloth. The bomb squad guy was now walking toward us with larger pieces of cloth.

Just then one of the nurses came running out of the E.D. Apparently, she had received a phone call from a patient we had treated the day before. He was at home watching the news and saw the event unfold and he was on his way back in to the E.D. because he wanted to "clear something up."

He arrived a few minutes later and was met by the police, the COO, and me. He started off by telling us how happy he was with the care he had received the day before. (I actually remember thinking to myself, "I hope he fills out a survey.") He wanted to do something nice for the team. He told the nurse who took care of him the day before what he did for a living and that he wanted to send something to the E.D. to say thanks. Unfortunately, she had called in sick this day so we didn't have that bit of information.

Apparently this nice man owned a scrub company and had sent over a hug box of scrubs, in all shapes, colors, and designs, for the E.D. staff. His delivery man was double-parked and in a rush so he ran into the E.D. and handed the box to the first nurse he saw, which turned out to be the ever-vigilant, and extremely dramatic, Dina.

"I just wanted to do something nice for you guys, and I am so sorry that all of this happened," he said as he pointed toward the parking lot of physician cars that were now covered with cute pictures of kitties, cartoon characters, and angels.

He was very upset. We and the police assured him that he was in no trouble. He was a nice guy and even went so far as to go to his truck and bring us over another box of scrubs. You'll be happy to hear that we didn't blow that box up. After all of the reports were filled out, we were now laughing about the day's events and saying our good-byes.

Our maintenance team was out with leaf blowers clearing out the debris from the doctors' cars and sending pebbles flying everywhere, which sent my COO running over there waving her arms. I shook the nice man's hand and thanked him for coming over to clear up the mystery.

"My goodness, I am so sorry," he said, looking at my elbow. "Were you hurt when they blew up the box?"

I thought for a second. No one was around us. "Yes," I said. "Yes I was. It's no big deal, just some debris hit me, you know."

He looked at me for a second and asked, "You were struck by flying scrub material?"

"No," I admitted. "I lied. It's embarrassing. Actually, I fell to the ground when I was startled by someone dropping something and hit my arm on a wheelchair."

Patting me on the shoulder he said, with sincerity, "Well, you are very brave."

That was nice of him.

INSPIRATION DESTINATION: APPRECIATE HUMOR.

SPIRITUAL STRETCH #1: What so often sustains us is humor. It has rescued the soul of many a person. Think about how good laughter is for you. I have read many studies and heard countless anecdotal stories about how humor has healed, elevated, and refreshed.

Think about the role humor plays in your life as a nurse. Do you laugh when something that you wouldn't normally wear ends up spilled on you? Can you see the humor in situations in your workplace? Can you think about ways that you can appropriately introduce humor into your world?

Today, your destination is laughter. Bring some into your working environment. Cut out cute cartoons for your coworkers. Bring in a funny book to lend to someone. Download jokes to tell to your patients. Talk with the team about having a "laugh room" or "laugh box" for your patients where they can borrow funny movies, books, or the like.

I saw this done on an oncology unit. There were dozens of DVDs of funny movies and comedy concerts. Laughter gets the endorphins flowing. It is healing stuff. Today is all about laughter, humor, and joy. What can you do to make that a part of your experience today?

Maybe you can create a time to share humor in faculty or staff meetings. Yes, we're in a serious business, and yes, we need to take what we do very seriously. But it's also okay to laugh. You need it. Your patients need it. Your staff needs it. Your students need it. Your soul needs it.

Inspiration will suffocate if it does not breathe in joy.

SPIRITUAL STRETCH #2: Using your journal, write down what you think is funny. Who is your favorite comedic actor or actress? What movies make you laugh? Who is the funniest person you know? Who makes you laugh at work? Who always has a funny joke to tell, an embarrassing story, or great witty comebacks? Is it you? Ponder what laughter means to you.

We have two choices in life. We laugh or we cry. Sometimes we laugh so hard that we cry; sometimes we cry so much we eventually start to laugh at how ridiculous the situation is.

Knowing that laughter and tears are often interchangeable, think about how you can choose laughter. Do you take yourself so seriously that you've become rigid? How can you make humor a mainstay? Can you or the team that you are on this journey with find a way to make this an "everyday" thing? Wouldn't life be better if laughter were a part of it?

CHAPTER

INSPIRATION DESTINATION:
SHARE THE INSPIRATION —
INSPIRE IT FORWARD

FOGGY MIRRORS

I once worked with a nurse who would never gossip. Never.

I would see groups of coworkers get together and start talking about someone we knew and each time I noticed that she would somehow remove herself from the group. I always admired that about her.

One day as we walked to the parking lot together, I stopped her and told her that I really respected that about her. She smiled and said, "Rich, some of these folks feel like if they can keep talking about others, the hot air from their breath will keep the mirror so fogged up they won't have to see their own reflection. What a shame they don't use that time to look for the good in others, like you just did right now. Do you do that enough?"

Wow. After we parted I sat in my car for a few minutes in the parking lot and thought about her words. I almost hadn't mentioned anything to her. She had just given me a huge compliment, but I was so far from being this "enlightened being" who looked for only the good in others. In fact, I felt totally undeserving of her praise.

Sometimes I found myself among those very same "talkative" folks, and while I wasn't the biggest gossip in the world, I was nothing close to being a saint either.

Her words had a great impact on me. I felt convicted, exposed. First, this conversation showed me the value of looking for the good in others, and second it reminded me that my mirror was also fogged because I was not, and still am not, where I would like to be. Third, it reminded me that when we "inspire it forward" there is much more given to us than we give away.

In other words, I needed to share the good, pass along the positive, and let people know that they make a difference by their example. What a wake-up call!

INSPIRATION DESTINATION: SHARE THE INSPIRATION. INSPIRE IT FORWARD.

SPIRITUAL STRETCH #1: What if there is good inside you and it only ever stays there? If there is music in your heart, or laughter in your spirit, who does it help if it always stays hidden? Remember the parable about the lantern kept under a bushel. If its light is hidden, to whom does it show the way? Get it?

So, if you feel a sense of inspiration, *inspire it forward*. Who comes to mind that could use a boost in spirit? Do you work with anyone who once had that glowing spirit and through life circumstance, or work stressors, lost it?

Often the best way to learn is to teach. By extension, the best way to become inspired is to inspire another.

Find a nurse you work with or are friends with and tell her one thing that you feel that she does very well. This is not a "thank-you note"— though you certainly may choose to send one later if you like. Think of this as an acknowledgment of her inspiring self.

Compliment her assessment skills, ability to run a meeting, organization skills, professional appearance, or willingness to help others. Stop her in the hall or catch her in her office or in the parking lot and start off by saying: "There's something about you that I find very inspirational and I need to tell you about it..."

After you have done this, observe her reaction. Watch her body language or simply listen to the words she chooses to thank you with. You will notice a light in her eyes.

Perhaps you could share with her why you are doing this. Let her know that you are trying to "inspire it forward." Mention that you have recently made a conscious choice to look for the good in those you work with. Maybe you will have inspired her to do the same.

Imagine what it would be like if this phenomenon took flight? Imagine if this circled through your hospital, office, or campus? Imagine the force of good that could be created?

Imagine if *all* of our mirrors became a little less foggy?

SPIRITUAL STRETCH #2: The cliché about the ripple effect of a pebble tossed into a pond and its profound impact is a great metaphor for *inspiring it forward*. This is different from rewarding and recognizing someone, because inspiring others sets the expectation that it will be followed up on and passed forward. Another truth that applies here is *good news travels fast*.

Follow up with the one you spoke with and ask her if she has inspired it forward. Ask to whom. What was the reaction? Create conversations about inspiration in your world.

CHAPTER 17

INSPIRATION DESTINATION:
PERFORM AN ANONYMOUS ACT OF KINDNESS

MIKE AND HIS MAGICAL BAG OF QUARTERS

My friend Mike was an unusual guy. I met him in New York City when I lived there during my early college days. He was tremendously positive about everything. He not only turned lemons into lemonade, he also made lemon meringue pie and lemon sorbet! The guy was inspiring to be around.

One day we met up for lunch. Mike bounded into the restaurant with his usual big grin. He tossed his hat and scarf down on the table and gave the waitress a huge smile. She gave him a huge smile back. I had been there for fifteen minutes and she had barely acknowledged me. Mike was magical like that.

"We're going to do something really cool today," he said. I tried to pry it out of him but he just kept saying, "You'll see."

When lunch was done Mike reached into his coat pocket and handed me a small bag of quarters. He plopped a second bag just like the first on the table in front of him. There had to be about ten dollars worth in each bag. I figured we were going to go play video games. I was psyched. I loved pinball.

"We're going to save some lives today," Mike told me with a serious look on his face.

Great. My eighteen-year-old brain was thinking more along the lines of Ms. Pac-Man than Mother Teresa. We made our way to some random city street that Mike had already scouted out. He stood there looking at me—like I had any idea whatsoever what we were there to do.

"We're going to find all of the expired meters we can and we're going to put in a quarter," he explained. "Whoever finishes first wins. There's bonus points if you put one in right as a meter maid is about to write a ticket."

He had to be kidding. It was Mike, though, so probably not!

I asked him how that was going to save lives. Mike took a long hard look at me. It was the kind of look you give someone who doesn't get a really easy-to-understand punch line. "Can you imagine what will happen to some of these people if they go home with a ticket?" he said, continuing much more dramatically, "Marriages will end, fortunes will be lost, lives will be at risk!"

I didn't know what to say. People were staring at these two guys holding bags of quarters. And it takes a lot for people to stare in New York City, trust me.

"Ready, set, go!"

Mike took off. He found the first two expired meters right away. I realized that it didn't make sense for me to be running behind him on the same side of the street because I was eating his dust. I crossed the street and narrowly missed getting killed by a cab.

I found my first meter almost immediately. Mike started screaming like a mad man from across the street, "Meter maid! Meter maid!" He ran ahead of the meter maid and found her target. He popped in two quarters into the meter that was in her sights. She just shook her head.

I saw another meter maid on my side of the road. She looked my way. She looked nervous. I saw her talking on the radio. I think her partner across the street was warning her. It was on.

Mike started yelling, "We're on the same side now, Rich. It's us against them! Give them nothing! Deprive them of victory!"

We were running along like nuts and laughing so hard we could hardly breathe. Sometimes we would skip a meter or two and have to backtrack. It was amazing how many meters were expired.

The meter maids were not happy with us. They gunned the engines of their meter maid carts. We were defeating them! Then suddenly they turned down another street and fled. Clearly, they were not as committed to victory as we were. The battle was ours.

At this point my quarters ran out. I noticed that Mike was already at the end of his block talking with a tall man in a really nice suit standing next to a Bentley. The man had his hand on Mike's shoulder. I ran across the street thinking that maybe Mike had scratched the guy's car or something and he was about to get in some kind of trouble.

By the time I crossed the street the man was getting into his car. I heard only one word of the conversation. As the man got into his car, he looked at me and he said, "Remarkable."

As he drove away, I turned to Mike. He had a big grin on his face. He was in "Mike-Heaven." "Check this out, dude!" Mike was holding two pieces of paper and he was handing one to me.

The man had given Mike two one-hundred-dollar bills.

That's right. This generous man had seen Mike and me running back and forth down the street, and he and some others were marveling at these two kids filling meters for no reason other than to help out strangers. (Okay, and to tick off the meter maids!) He told Mike it gave him hope for the future to see us do what we were doing and he wanted to thank us.

We were now officially rich. I was also very lucky. None of this had been my idea. I was simply a fortunate beneficiary of the huge heart and infinite love for the world that Mike had.

Ultimately, I lost track of Mike, as we sometimes do with friends of our youth. He was a unique person. I bet he's out there somewhere right now, filling someone's meter, or picking up someone's trash, or pulling someone's Sunday paper out of a puddle.

I remember feeling absolutely on top of the world that day. Sure, the hundred dollars was a huge windfall for a kid in 1986, but it was really more the sheer joy of doing some anonymous act of kindness that did it. That day will be with me forever.

INSPIRATION DESTINATION:
PERFORM AN ANONYMOUS ACT OF KINDNESS.

SPIRITUAL STRETCH #1: Be like Mike by doing something nice for someone without letting her know you did it. Why does your act of kindness have to be anonymous? Because the inspiration is not in getting a thank-you or even a hundred-dollar surprise. The inspiration is in the simple act of the kindness. That's it. You will walk away from this feeling as if you and the universe share some sweet, beautiful secret. It is the neatest exercise.

There are a million ways you can do this. Bring a neighbor's garbage can in for him on a rainy day. Run the labs down for the unit secretary or tech before they do it. Give the free lunch ticket you received at work for your birthday to the cafeteria cashier and ask her to comp someone's lunch. Use your imagination.

You can perform your anonymous act at work or at home. Look for the opportunity today. I guarantee it will present itself to you. Maybe you can even make this a daily habit. Imagine if just 0.1 percent of the people in the world did this. Imagine if there were even five people at work who did this.

It is inspiring to make a difference. It is inspiring to help. It is inspiring to be in it for nothing more than to be in it.

Fill someone's meter today.

SPIRITUAL STRETCH #2: You may have noticed that giving is an ongoing theme in this book, whether it is giving to self or others. There is such a powerful energy in the act of giving. Everything I have read about inspiration while researching for this book included some aspect of giving. Why is that, do you think?

Ask yourself that question. Journal about it. I have some thoughts on why and I have shared some in this book, but yours will be different from mine.

This is your journey. How do you give? In what ways do you find inspiration in giving? Is it easy or hard for you to be anonymous when you give? Learn about yourself. Dig deeper. Really chew on this for a while. What can you discover about yourself and inspiration as it relates to giving?

CHAPTER 18

INSPIRATION DESTINATION:
GIVE OF YOUR TIME AND KNOWLEDGE

EL LOCO INFERMERO DE AMERICA (THE CRAZY NURSE FROM AMERICA)

One of the most rewarding times in my nursing life was when I went on a medical mission to Honduras with my church. It still amazes me how those several days changed me forever.

I had never felt so inspired than when I was in that hot and humid "clinic" in the middle of a faraway village surrounded by the most beautiful and appreciative people I had ever met. It was a humbling experience.

I struggled with being able to communicate, as my Spanish falls somewhere between "horrible" and "pathetic." But every time I got frustrated with myself, someone came along to tell me to *relax and trust*.

These are not things I do easily. I tend to be wired more toward "anxious" than "relaxed"! But there was a lesson for me here. I had to go slowly. I had to speak slowly. Being frustrated with myself would serve no one. I had to be in the moment. I had to be purposeful. And I succeeded—which led to some of the most inspirational and fulfilling experiences of my life.

I remember the service held in the village's hand-built church. I cried. We all did. It was that beautiful. I remember the flowers on the altar neatly placed in their humble vases made of halved two-liter soda bottles. The shy smiles of the children. The respectful acknowledgment of the elders.

Also, I remember the polite laughter when I, a guy born in Brooklyn and raised in urban Miami, attempted to ride a horse like a cowboy and instead backed it into a barbed-wire fence tearing my scrubs and my leg. Hey...I didn't know how to say "Whoa" in Spanish!

Once, after we had completed our work in the clinic, I tried to help them bring in the livestock from the field and didn't realize that the really big and stubborn cow with the horns was actually not a cow at all, but a bull. They don't like being pushed, apparently. That was fun.

Everyone was screaming for me to run as the bull began to snort and kick the dirt. They couldn't believe I could run that fast. I couldn't believe I could run that fast. We all had a good laugh. It was outside of my element, for sure, and I loved it. It changed me and opened my eyes. It made me more grateful for many things.

Also, it made me realize how selfish I was. I had to hold up the mirror quite a bit when I was there. I didn't always like what I saw.

Yes, my trip to Honduras may have earned me the label *El loco Infermero de America* (the crazy nurse from America). But it also helped make me an inspired nurse. It brought me back yet again to what Quint

Studer speaks so eloquently about: *Purpose, Worthwhile Work and Making a Difference.* And that's worth any number of misadventures with livestock!

INSPIRATION DESTINATION: GIVE OF YOUR TIME AND KNOWLEDGE.

SPIRITUAL STRETCH #1: Now perhaps braving jungles, large spiders, ice cold showers, and angry bulls is not for you. That's okay. But there must be some way you can give back. And while you may not be able to start your volunteer work today, you can plan it, look for it, talk about it with your peers or friends, ask questions, journal about it, inquire about it, and put the wheels in motion.

You will be really amazed at what may come up today. Someone may tell you about a health fair she is volunteering at the next week and you might just happen to be off that day. Or you may choose to contact your place of worship and find that there's a need for you to help with free blood pressure screenings or lectures on diabetes.

Often the best way to connect to your passion is to give of yourself and your time. And there are infinite ways to do this. What better way is there to be inspired than to see the appreciation in the eyes of someone that you have helped, for no other reason than because you cared? Not as part of your job, or for pay, or even for a pat on the back...just because.

Inspiration is built into the act of giving. I would venture to say that inspiration is at its very *core*. Giving of your time and expertise serves the dual purpose of inspiring self and inspiring others. The caring heart that you possess as a nurse needs to be fed. Not doing so deprives you of the fuel you need to sustain your spirit in this field.

Give back to others. It is often the best way to give to yourself.

SPIRITUAL STRETCH #2: Should the volunteer work you've looked into be a one-time gesture? It could be. And maybe that is enough. (If you're a busy single parent with three kids, for instance, it may *have* to be enough!) On the other hand, it could be the beginning of an ongoing commitment to serve others.

Don't feel constrained by your career. You may volunteer at something that has no connection whatsoever to nursing. You could mentor an at-risk teen, or hand out cold water at a walk-a-thon, or play the piano at a nursing home, or mow the lawn of a neighbor in need of help.

The idea here is for you to say to yourself: *Self, I am lending you to someone else to make his or her life a little better.* And then just do it.

CHAPTER 19

INSPIRATION DESTINATION:

MAKE A WHY-I'M-GRATEFUL-FOR-BEING-A-NURSE LIST

THE RED NOTEBOOK

I procrastinate. Sometimes, I procrastinate so much that it takes me a little while to get around to procrastinating. I also have Attention Deficit Disorder so I need help staying organized. (I'm pretty sure I had ADD as a kid. But they didn't call it ADD back then. They called it "detention.")

Actually, I do actually get a lot done for someone as distracted as I am, but it helps me to make lists. At least I thought it did. I read recently that lists are actually a *bad* idea for people who are prone to procrastinating, because the procrastinator spends her/his time writing the lists instead of doing the stuff on the lists, thus, procrastinating even more.

I was a little upset when I read that because I thought I found a good way to get organized. Well, I'm not actually sure if the article totally puts down lists because I got a little distracted when I was reading the article and I didn't actually read the entire thing—just the first part. But I tore it out of the magazine and I do plan on reading it in a little while when I get around to it. I actually added reading the article to my list of things I need to get done. Maybe I'll learn something. You never know where knowledge will come from.

(See what I mean? Now, on with the story!)

Ron was a successful businessman with a close-knit family. He was also a fit guy who worked out every day, which is what brought him into my life. One morning, while jogging, he was hit by a car and suffered several traumatic injuries.

I met Ron and his family during his road to recovery while he was undergoing rehabilitation. His wife sought me out to assist them with some legal papers while I was a director of risk management. His wife told me that Ron had partial paralysis of the right side of his body, had difficulty speaking, and could not yet walk without assistance.

When I went to Ron's room I expected to see a man at the low point of his life. To my surprise, he greeted me, extended his left hand, and said jokingly, "I don't like my right hand to know what my left hand is doing."

Frankly, I had expected someone a little less energetic and a little more depressed. Heck, I would've been.

As I went through all of the paperwork with them, he continued to tease and joke around. When we got to discussing some decisions about healthcare surrogates he joked, "I think my wife was the one driving the car that hit me. She was pretty mad at me for leaving the toilet seat up that morning. I don't know if I want her in charge of pulling the plug!" They both had a good laugh at that.

Ron's wife had to go pick up their six-year-old son from school, so I offered to sit with him for a few minutes. We got to talking about life and I had to ask him a question. "Ron, I hope you don't mind my asking you this, but how are you managing to stay so positive through all of this?"

He motioned to his side table where I noticed a red notebook. "Open that," he said. I did and I began to read.

Inside was a list and it covered dozens of pages. He told me that he had dictated some of it, but being a lefty he was able to write some as well.

"This is my list of reasons to keep going," Ron said. "I have a lot going against me right now. I haven't had a paycheck in two months. I may never regain some of my physical abilities and even some mental ones. My memory is not the same and they told me that they don't know what I will get back

"But if I live there, in that 'place of can't,' if I lay here thinking about that, what good is that going to do me?" he continued. "So, instead, my wife and I decided to list all of the reasons that I should go on—all the things that I am grateful for."

I couldn't believe how long the list was. "Go on," he said. "Read them."

There were so many items on the list. Ron had started each page with, "I am very grateful for..." and then on each line wrote a gratitude sentence. For example:

"That I was jogging the morning I was hit rather than biking with Jake (his little boy) riding in the child seat."

"That I had purchased long-term disability insurance."

"That my wife is beautiful."

"Chocolate cake."

It went on and on. He listed things great and small, serious and silly. He was grateful for his surgeons. He was grateful that he set the timer on his sprinklers two days before his accident so his wife wouldn't have to. He was grateful for a private room in rehabilitation. He was grateful that his business partner ordered catered meals to be sent to his home for his wife and son so they wouldn't have to worry about grocery shopping and cooking.

"If I keep my mind focused on what I am grateful for, I won't allow my thoughts to drift to all that I am worried about," he explained. "I can't afford that. I need to heal myself for my family. They need me. My friends need me. My customers need me. I can't be there for them and 'Mr. Regret' at the same time. I only have room for gratitude. Not regret."

His wife soon returned with their son who gave his dad a big hug. "Guess what, Daddy?" the boy said, holding up a piece of paper. "I got all my spelling words right!"

"Wow!" exclaimed Ron. "Hey, Rich, grab my list—that's another one to add!"

We wrote it down. His wife also told him to add that she found a front row parking spot, so the list grew by two items even in the few minutes I was there.

After we said our good-byes, I took the long way back to my office. I had some thinking to do. This experience really caused me to do some introspection. Where did I focus my thoughts? Just that morning I had a personal meltdown because I found a nail in my tire and had to stop on my way to work to get it plugged. Was that really such a big deal?

Also, my wonderful son was healthy, I was healthy, my wife was healthy, I could use my arms and legs and my memory was great, and I had a great job...yet I was whining about a nail, while someone like Ron was facing down a lifetime of struggle by looking for the good and filling his mind with gratitude.

I was, once again, in awe of what the folks I encountered in my nursing career could teach me. There are such great lessons out there, aren't there? I had never thought of using a list for such a thing.

Sure, you could use a list to remind you to pick up a loaf of bread, but I never thought you could use a list to pick up your spirits. I made a list that night. It felt good.

From time to time, when I feel like I am in need of elevation, I make a gratitude list. I always think of Ron. Sometimes when you least expect to learn something, you do.

INSPIRATION DESTINATION: MAKE A WHY-I'M-GRATEFUL-FOR-BEING-A-NURSE LIST.

SPIRITUAL STRETCH #1: We use lists a lot. The purpose of a list, to most people, is to write or type out things that we need to get or to get done so that we can stay on task and also so we can remember things.

Often, lists make things very tangible. When you list out what you want to get done, for example, you may find that you've added too much to the day and you need to cut back. When you can "see" something in front of your eyes, it helps you to understand it better. You can make more progress and map out a plan. Maybe it can be the same for gratitude and inspiration.

Today you will make your destination for inspiration about *gratitude*. You've probably heard about gratitude lists before. Well, now is the time to make one. And I want you to give it a different spin. I want you to focus on what you are most grateful for as it relates to being a nurse.

What do you love about being a nurse? What are the best parts? What keeps you going? What does a good day look like? Start off the list by writing, "As a nurse I am very grateful for..." and then go at it.

There is nothing too big or too small. It might be that you love wearing "pajamas" to work, as one friend noted referring to her scrubs, rather than having to fuss over uncomfortable suits and skirts. It might be that you save lives, help people, relieve pain. Be general and be specific.

Your destination is to realize that you have much to be inspired about *already* in your nursing life. It is right in front of you.

You do worthwhile work as a nurse. Sure, your days can be long and the work can be hard, but you have a job. Some can only wish for the job security that many in nursing enjoy. Find gratitude. Focus on it. Be relentless in your pursuit of that which you are grateful for. Flood your mind and your journal with words of gratitude. This creates a "grateful plateful" upon which your inspiration will feed.

Sometimes when we feel like our passion has dipped or we feel discouraged, it is easy to focus on the nail in the tire. But think this way: You have three tires that don't have a nail. You didn't blow a tire going seventy miles per hour and wreck your car. Be grateful for that.

Gratitude will lead you to inspiration. Inspiration will increase your gratitude. It is a beautiful circle.

Walk the path paved with words of written thanks. It will lead you to places you have only dreamed about.

SPIRITUAL STRETCH #2: Do you sometimes feel that if you talk about what you are grateful for it will be taken from you, or perhaps that it will make you sound "full of yourself"? Some of us may have been raised that way. We are actually afraid of gratitude! Isn't that mindboggling?

Challenge yourself here to break through that fear. This is about being grateful for the good in your nursing life, not about you having more power or being smarter or making more money than "another nurse." So there is no "conceit" involved. Practice being fearlessly grateful for what you do, see, hear, and experience as a nurse

CHAPTER
20

INSPIRATION DESTINATION:
WATCH YOUR MOUTH!
(USE NEW WORDS.)

JOSIE'S NIGHT OFF

This was going to be one of "those nights." I sensed it as soon as the doors to the unit opened. I was in charge that night and I arrived to a full unit of very sick patients.

Aside from that, there was a coup in the making. Josie was the driving force. She was what I would refer to as a psychic vampire. You know the type? They suck the joy out of your soul.

The first voice I heard was Josie's. "This night better not be as bad as the one I had last week when you were in charge." Nice.

Josie was not a full-time staff member. She did occasional shifts to "help us out." Yet, what she really "helped" with was making her peers miserable.

She complained endlessly. She answered every question from across the room. She deplored your politics and beliefs. She hated all the movies or books that you liked and told you that the diet/exercise program/ church/temple/marriage/lifesaving surgery that you found some joy in or had faith in would serve no purpose and would fail to meet even the least of your expectations.

Are you with me? Can you feel my pain? Don't you want Josie to come work with you?

Back to the story. I smiled at Josie, clutching my coffee. I began to make the assignments to the best of my ability, matching up the nurses with the patients they had the night before. That's how we did it. It seemed to be what worked for everyone. Well, everyone except Josie, that is.

You see, Josie was the one exception to the "same assignment they had before" rule that day. Why? Because she had not *been* at work the night before. (I don't know where she'd been; I assume she was off somewhere studying up on charge nurse torture methods.)

Anyway, she said, "*Of course* he gives me the worst assignment. Typical. I don't know why I come back here. This place is the worst."

She was in rare form. I had consumed only half a cup of coffee at this point. This could get ugly, I thought.

I calmly explained why I made the assignments the way I did. A few other staff members weighed in on my "side." Luckily we were not at all in hearing range of any patients. Josie would hear none of it. She started to take out her frustrations on the nurse giving her report. Nothing was good enough for her.

She went on a rampage about how horrible the care was, how no one works together and how if she was in charge instead of "him" the world would be a better place. The room was suddenly dark. Josie's negativity darkened everyone's mood. This was going to be a long night.

Suddenly, I heard a voice. It said, "Josie, go ahead and go home. We'll be fine without you tonight."

Who said that?

"What? Who will take my assignment?" asked Josie.

The voice continued, "I will take your assignment, Josie. Thanks for coming in. You can leave."

Oh my. The voice was mine. Did I just say that? Josie literally stood there for a good minute staring at me in disbelief. I think she threatened my life for a while but eventually she grabbed her bag, made one last attempt to convince me that we couldn't possibly survive without her and then—thankfully—she left.

So, I took her assignment. It wasn't easy but I managed my charge duties and the rest of the team as always, helped each other (and me) out. The world turned and we were just fine. As a matter of fact, we had a great shift. People were smiling. You began to hear different words being spoken.

The negativity had left our space. It was amazing! The words that she used had sucked the life out of us. The endless negative mantra coming from this person created a cloud of doom—and we had allowed it.

A bunch of us got together after that night and reflected on the "Josie factor." What came out of this conversation was that the "power" that Josie had over us, while 100 percent in our heads, was nothing more than the words of a bully. Her negativity formed a fence around us. We were literally imprisoned by her words. They darkened the room and changed our moods. We argued more when she worked.

Now, don't get me wrong, we do claim *some* ownership here, but it was incredible to see how the words she used had this power over us. We pledged that instead of turning on Josie and ignoring her, we would try to battle darkness with light.

So when she worked again, I approached her and extended my hand. I told her I was sorry for how things went last time we worked and that I wanted us to have a better working relationship. I asked what I could do to contribute to this. She thought for a moment and said, "You could listen better." I didn't defend myself. I could listen better. She was right.

I swallowed my ego and said, "Okay, I will." I waited for her to ask what she could do to contribute but I realized that I might have to encourage that. "Josie, can I ask something of you in return?"

She replied, "Okay, shoot."

I answered, "Could you try to be a bit more positive. To be honest, I am not asking you to change who you are or how you think, because frankly that is none of my concern, but can you just change what you say? Because I can hear the words you choose to say. They are my concern. They affect me."

Now, I should be really honest here. I wanted to say "us" but I didn't want to come across as the "spokesmodel" for the team. I kept it about Josie and me.

She thought for a moment and then tilted her head with a smile. "I'm a big mouth. This isn't the first time someone told me to watch my mouth. I know I'm not easy to get along with but I appreciate you being honest with me. I will work on it, deal?"

"Deal," I responded.

And guess what? She did work on it. She got better, for a while. Then she took a travel assignment and left town. I missed her.

Okay, that's not true. I actually didn't miss her, but I did learn from her. A wise person once told me that you often learn more from the difficult people in your life than you do from the "nice" ones. I think it is true.

Words make a difference.

INSPIRATION DESTINATION: WATCH YOUR MOUTH! (USE NEW WORDS.)

SPIRITUAL STRETCH #1: Words are powerful things. They heal nations. They change lives. What words do you use? Do you use words like "fried," "burnt," "tired," "overworked," "stressed," and the like? You can *hear* yourself. You can also *heal* yourself.

Today, make an effort to change your vocabulary. If your goal here is to be inspired, it is a full-on tactile experience. What you say influences how you feel. I have heard it called "self-talk." Today you will speak the language of inspiration. Use phrases and words that have that feel to them. Here are a very few examples:

1. "This is one of those really good days."
2. "I'm looking forward to a good day today."
3. "We're going to have a great shift; I can feel it."
4. "It's all good today."
5. "I'm doing great...it's good to see you."
6. "We have a great team on today."
7. "I am glad to see you. The day always goes smoothly when you're here."
8. "I would be happy to help you out—you are always there for me."
9. "Thanks so much for doing that; you are wonderful."
10. "Night shift did a great job last night. My patient was raving about her nurse. There are some superstars working here."

If none of these appeal to you, that's okay. This is not meant to be a literal list. I included it just to get you started. I live in the real world. I know when you "read" stuff like this it can sound a bit "fluffy." I think there are two reasons for this. First, our ears and our minds are not wired toward the positive. The media and the "cool kids" always make fun of anything positive. And second, when you see this as the written word, you lose the inflection and the personal connection. The real emotion gets a little lost in translation.

So choose words that won't embarrass you or make you self-conscious. Just make sure they're words other than "Josie" words. The idea is to acknowledge that there is great power in words—and strive to use better ones.

Your soul is listening. Watch your mouth!

SPIRITUAL STRETCH #2: Try this experiment. I did and it was surprising. Keep a small piece of paper or pad with you. Write down every descriptive word that you say. At the end of the day, read it.

Do you say things like "good," "beautiful," "perfect"...and if you do, are you being real or sarcastic? Do you say things like "stupid," "useless," "horrible"? What does your language say about you?

How do you speak about yourself? "I'm such a loser" or "I can't do anything right." Or, "I am really good at this" and "I'm having a great day." How do you talk about others? "He's a mess!" or "I can't stand when I have to call him." Or "She is so smart" and "I love when he's here."

Words are powerful things. What kind of power do yours project?

CHAPTER

21

INSPIRATION DESTINATION:
CREATE AFFIRMATIONS AND USE
THEM TO CHANGE YOUR LIFE

THE PICTURE ON THE REFRIGERATOR

One day, my wife and I went to a friend's house to pick him up for a birthday party. He was still getting ready, so we made ourselves at home. My wife wandered into the kitchen and she called me to come in there. She wanted me to see something.

On his refrigerator were a dozen or so neatly written sentences. Some were quotes. Others were sentences written as if he were speaking to himself. One said, "I am fit and in shape. I am healthy and strong. My body is a blessing."

There was also a picture on the refrigerator. It looked like maybe it could be my friend's older brother—a much heavier older brother.

As we were looking at the notes and the picture, my friend came into the kitchen. "Oh, I see you found some of my affirmations," he said. "I have them everywhere–in my bathroom, in my car, pretty much everywhere. I know it may seem weird but it really helps me."

I found this fascinating. I was about to ask him more about the affirmations when my wife said, "Who is this guy in the picture? He looks like you, but I didn't know you had a brother."

"Oh no, that is me. Well, it *was* me, about 160 pounds ago!"

We were astonished. My friend couldn't have been more than 150 pounds. It seemed he had lost half his previous body weight! It was amazing.

"How did you lose all of that weight?" I asked.

He invited us to sit down. He was quiet for a second, and then he began to tell his story:

> "I was always an unhealthy and overweight kid. My dad was very abusive and would tease me about being overweight. The more he did, the more I ate. My mom left him when I was still young, but the words that he used still lived in my head. They became my words.
>
> "I hated being unhealthy. I hated feeling bad about myself. No matter what I tried—diets, pills, personal trainers—it would only work for awhile and then I would fall into the same patterns.
>
> "It was more than just watching what I ate. I also got myself into major debt. I used shopping to feel better. I would buy things that I neither needed nor could afford. I bought expensive gifts for 'friends' in the hopes that they would like me. It was sad, but I didn't know any better.

"I keep the picture of my former self on the refrigerator to remind me of who I once was. I remember where I was when that picture was taken. It was at a party. There was someone there I had a major crush on. As my friend took the picture, a guy who was standing with my 'crush' yelled out, 'You better use the wide lens!'

"Everyone started laughing. It was a painful moment. Once again the cruel words that people can use crept into my head. It wasn't about just being overweight, as I believe there is beauty in people of all shapes and sizes. It was about allowing myself to be 'abused' and about abusing myself as well. See, I had internalized what others said about me and it became my own self-talk.

"On that day I decided that while I couldn't control the cruelty of others and I had no power over how others would speak to me, I *did* have power and control of what I let in and what I let out. So the next day I was in a bookstore and I came across a book about affirmations. They are simply phrases that you say to yourself to affirm good things like, 'I have much abundance in my life and I am grateful for it' or 'I am a lovable person and I attract love into my life.' Things like that.

"I began using them and it started me on a very different road. Through speaking differently and 'coaching' myself with positive and motivating words, I began to have different pictures in my head. I began seeing and believing that I was meant to be happy and healthy, and I have not turned back since.

"Affirmations are simply conversations with yourself. They allow better, positive, and affirming words to take over space in your head. I am not saying that I simply had to start talking to myself—don't get me wrong. But what I learned was, no matter how hard I exercised, no matter how strict I was with my diet, I still *believed* that I was an overweight and unhealthy person so nothing worked for long. Even when I would lose some weight, I still heard 'voices' in my head telling me I was ugly or useless or that I would never amount to anything.

"It sounds a bit crazy, but when I took control over what words my mind heard, it changed my soul as well. I felt better.

"The words created images in my mind. The images inspired me to achieve my goals. I began seeing progress and I got more fired up to keep going. Within a year or so, I got healthier and the weight came off. I stopped spending and I worked overtime and got an extra job to get out of debt.

"It all changed for me when I changed how I spoke to myself and made a conscious effort to comfort that little kid that still lives inside me that never heard words of praise or support. I had to be the one to do it."

He paused and looked seriously at our stunned faces. "Did I just ramble on and bore you?"

Neither my wife nor I spoke. We both stood up and gave our friend a big hug. Needless to say, there were quite a few notes stuck up on my walls that next week. I was inspired.

What an amazing story! Here was a man who came from a horrible upbringing, who had been physically and emotionally abused, and who somehow found the tools to climb out of that. His healing was augmented by reading, counseling, and a lot of introspection.

Affirmations were one of the tools that led him toward success and joy. He still uses them today. Just so you know: Yes, the weight is still off. Yes, he is out of debt, healthy, and in a great relationship.

Yes, he still has the picture on the refrigerator. It's now in a magnetic frame that reads, "I love you." That's the ultimate affirmation.

INSPIRATION DESTINATION: CREATE AFFIRMATIONS AND USE THEM TO CHANGE YOUR LIFE.

SPIRITUAL STRETCH #1: Have you noticed that what you tell yourself often happens? You spill your coffee on your shirt in the morning and you say aloud, "Great, this is how my day is going to go, I can just feel it." Then you back out and run over your garbage pail, which dents your car. You get out of your car and say to yourself, "Nice! I knew this day would stink. Can't wait for the next disaster!" Then you get to work and realize you left your wallet at home and you don't have any lunch money, to which you exclaim to all who are near and far, "My life stinks!" On and on it goes.

Do you have days like that? Now, don't think for a second that I am saying that it is only what you say to yourself that is the cause of all of these calamities, but can you see even a slight connection? What you say affects how you feel, which affects how your life goes.

While this is similar to what we talked about in the Inspiration Destination that focused on words (Chapter 20), I want you to be more proactive here. This is about using affirmations. I define affirmations as purposeful self-talk in which you affirm a positive outlook or outcome for your life. When you do this on a regular basis, it feeds your mind.

Here's a basic how-to for affirmations.

- Get some index cards. If they are too boring, use your computer to make some fancier "cards" on which you will print your affirmations. Sticky notes work, too. You want your affirmations to be written and placed in such a way that you have easy access to them and can "use" them at least daily.

- Think about what you want to change or improve in your life. This can be personal or nursing-related, but as you are on the journey for inspiration in your nursing life, make at least a few affirmations specific to that. You may want to feel healthier, more confident, more in touch with Spirit. You may want to be more caring, improve your work or personal relationships, or have an overall more positive outlook. What do you want to affect for the better? How can you be more inspired? Make a list. Think it over. There's no wrong or right here.

- After you have settled on your list of that which you want to change or improve, think about how you can state the affirmations. For example, let's say on your list you wrote that you want to have more peace in your work life. You could write the following affirmation: "I am peaceful. I am surrounded by peace. Peace flows through me. There is peace in all that I do, all that I hear, all that I say, and in all whom I meet. I am peaceful today." State this in the positive and use "I" phrases like "I am." I prefer to state them as if they are true or have happened already, rather than stating that they are going to be true at a later time like "I hope." That has worked for me. Keep your affirmations short, positive, and easy to remember. Write a few drafts. Get comfortable with them. You will know it when it works.

- Write your affirmations on your index cards or sticky notes. Remember, these affirmations are for you to read each day so think about how you can make them accessible. I know someone who painted hers on a small canvas and hung it in her bathroom. It looks good and it allows her to read them each morning as she gets ready. You can make more than one of the same affirmation so that one goes in your purse or wallet, one goes on your bathroom mirror, and one goes in your briefcase. You can make them scroll across your computer screen or pop up on your cell phone when you turn it on.

- When you say these affirmations, it is most effective to say them aloud. At some point they will be memorized. When you read them, say them, and hear yourself say them, you are activating many of your senses. This makes them come alive for you.

- Feel and see what you are saying. That is, make these words real. If you are speaking about peace, then see peace in your mind and feel peace in your body. If you are speaking about health, then feel healthy. See and feel yourself feeling good, strong, confident, in shape, or whatever "healthy" means to you. It is one of the most powerful experiences that you can have to align your words, your mind, and your senses.

- Make this a habit. If you live alone, give yourself permission to talk to yourself. If you live with others, ask their indulgence and speak freely, or if you choose, take time to be alone. If you feel anyone might make fun of you, keep that out of your experience. This is for you. You are talking to you. Feed your inspiration with healthy words that affirm that which you believe would enhance your journey.

- Make this a part of your day. Each day. This is like being on an inspirational exercise program. The more you do it, the better the outcome. Do your affirmations in your car, in the shower, during your walks to the pharmacy, or when you jog, walk, bike, or do exercise.

- Feel "good" when you say them. Clear your mind. Feed it with the powerful positive images that you wish to achieve be they health, love, or abundance.

As we discussed when we talked about words earlier, there is great power in the words that we choose to speak to others. We also hear what we say. Those words affect our moods and our thoughts. I would venture to say that, even more, the words we speak directly to ourselves can be life-changing and inspirational.

Add affirmations to your inspiration journey. Having these daily conversations with "you" will help you grow your inspiration from the inside out.

SPIRITUAL STRETCH #2: Take your study of affirmations to the next level. There are many, many resources out there. Go online and read about them or buy a book about affirmations. Journal about the things you would like to make affirmations about. If you are in school, maybe write a paper about affirmations. Have fun with this. Enjoy having some affirming conversations with yourself. You will be inspired by what you experience.

CHAPTER

INSPIRATION DESTINATION:
MAKE AN INSPIRATION PLAN

THE VICIOUS ARMADILLO

"What is all of that up there?" I asked Dan as we drove down a dark road somewhere between Lubbock, Texas, and Altus, Oklahoma. We were on our way from one of the hospitals that we were working with as Studer Group coaches to our next stop.

"Up where?" he asked, in the incredibly patient way he has about him. Dan was my preceptor as I was learning the ropes of being a coach with Studer Group. He is, in my mind, the all-around smartest person I know and also one of the best human beings you can meet.

I was referring to these huge glowing lights in the sky that looked like a blanket of flashbulbs. He slowed the car and pulled over to the side of the road. We were on something called a "farm road." That was new to me. I was a city boy. I think it was Farm Road 211.

It was around nine 'o clock at night, and we were literally in the middle of nowhere. I mean that. If you look up "the middle of nowhere" in the dictionary, it will say "Farm Road 211, Texas-ish." I say "Texas-ish" because I think we were still in the Lone Star state (a nickname, which, as you'll soon see, is ironic). I wasn't sure, which was scary because it was my job to navigate.

So, Dan pulled over and we got out. Thinking maybe I was seeing a UFO or something, Dan excitedly asked me again, "What did you see?" I pointed up at the night sky. "That blanket of lights, is that some weird meteor shower or something?"

Dan looked at me with a steady gaze. "No, Rich. That's the Milky Way."

"Oh, my goodness!" I said. "Why is it so bright? Is this some seasonal thing?"

"No, Rich, that's what it looks like when you are not in the city. Haven't you ever been camping?" he asked.

"Yes, I've been camping," I lied. "But, I think it was cloudy."

He laughed and we soon got back in the car. My job was simple. Other than checking the sky for UFOs, I was supposed to be reading the directions our wonderful coworker Stacy had downloaded for us onto our BlackBerries. They were good directions, but Dan and the Milky Way were obviously much brighter than me because I was struggling to keep up.

At one point, I asked Dan to shut the car lights off to see how dark it was. At first he looked at me like I was insane, but then he did shut off the lights for a second. We cracked up like two ten-year-olds.

Despite my attempts to distract Dan, he knew he had to get us to our destination. I had my eyes on the BlackBerry and I was doing my best to navigate. After a few minutes Dan said, "What was that?"

I looked up from the BlackBerry thinking that maybe he saw Big Foot or something. "What was what?" I asked.

"Did you see a sign?" Dan asked.

"No, we're good," I assured Dan. "The directions say to stay on Farm Road 211 until we get to 259 and then to make a right."

We drove for a minute, but something was bugging Dan. "I'm going to turn around." We did. Well, we tried. The car got temporarily stuck in the soft earth on the side of the road.

You can tell I am a city boy, because when I got out to check why we were stuck I used my cell phone light as a flashlight to see in the dark. I thought it was pretty smart. Dan thought it was hysterical.

Anyway, we got unstuck, which I was glad about, but suddenly I saw some glowing eyes in the bushes and this big animal came walking out. I screamed. It was an armadillo. I wasn't sure if they were vicious. Dan assured me they were not. It looked pretty mean. Don't laugh. It was big. I think it growled. I used my cell phone light to scare it away. It worked. I felt exonerated.

We got back in the car and back-tracked. I argued with Dan that I was sure we were on the right road because the BlackBerry said so. Sure enough, when we drove back a few miles, there was a sign. You could barely see it, but it was there. It read "Farm Road 259" with an arrow pointing to a small, barely visible crossroad.

I had missed it. Dan had not. He didn't rub it in. I think he understood that I was distracted by the fact that I had just learned that the Milky Way was more than my favorite snack. But, I learned something else from that trip. There was a difference between Dan and me—that was the key.

Dan had his eyes on the road. I had my eyes on something telling me where the road was. He was in the "now"; I was in the "vague." He knew the plan. I had the CliffsNotes.

It was a valuable lesson for me. I don't know about you, but sometimes I can be less than present. Sometimes I "wing it" when I should take a moment and thoughtfully plan my next steps. Sometimes I take my eye off of the road and crash hard because of it.

I will never forget that drive to nowhere. We made it safely to Oklahoma thanks to Dan.

The stars really do shine bright in Texas.

I'm still skeptical about the whole armadillo thing, though. I still think they might be more vicious than Dan realizes.

INSPIRATION DESTINATION: MAKE AN INSPIRATION PLAN.

SPIRITUAL STRETCH #1: Becoming more inspired won't be something that you stumble upon or luck into. You can't read this book, or go to a seminar, or find a four-leaf clover and hope for inspiration. You need to have a plan and you need to keep your "eyes on the road."

Today, make your plan. Use your journal to map it out. If you are working within a group, come up with a map together and decide how you can best support each other. Again, this is a creative process, but it won't hurt to be a little prescriptive too.

Decide specifically what your overall goal is. It may be "To be more inspired" or it may be "To inspire others." It may be "To feel more positive about my work, coworkers, or myself." What is your goal? Why are you reading this book?

Next, decide how you are going to measure your success. Maybe you can rate your "attitude" each day starting today on a 1-5 scale: "1" is poor and "5" is excellent as it relates to how you feel about your work and nursing. Set a goal. Make it reachable.

If you are a "1," decide that your goal is to be a "3" within, for example, 90 days. If you are a "3," strive for a "5." Of course, your ultimate goal is to be a "5" wherever you are, but you will get there. Set a goal that you can reach, and once you reach it, set another even higher.

If you don't like this system, come up with another way to measure your specific goal. Maybe track feedback from your peers or your loved ones. Maybe they can rate you. This is yours.

Next, after you have determined a goal and decided how you will measure it, decide upon the tactics that you will take to get there. Plan your tactics in increments, like 60 or 90 days. This part will be easy because you have plenty of tactics right here in this book.

Maybe you will focus on affirmations, honoring your mentor, using different words, and ten minutes of purpose as your tactics for the first 30 days. Write this out. This is your self-evaluation. This is your road to your ultimate Inspiration Destination.

After your time frame is up, reassess where you are. Did you achieve your goal? If not, what can you do differently? If you achieved your goal, how can you either improve further or hardwire your success? Be sure to make this your own, but below is an example of what it could look like:

Goal: To feel more inspired to a level of "4" during the course of my workday within 60 days.
Measurement: Using a 1-5 scale I will evaluate my "level of inspiration" on a daily basis. 1=completely uninspired, 2=barely inspired, 3=somewhat inspired, 4=inspired, 5= very inspired.
Tactics: I will focus on 5 tactics for a 60-day period. These will be: 1. Creating affirmations. 2. Writing a daily nursing gratitude list. 3. Honoring my mentor. 4. Supporting new nurses. 5. Being welcoming of spirit.

Take this to new levels. After 60 or 90 days, have a "meeting" with yourself or your team and check your progress. Talk or think about what has changed or what could be better. The idea here is to not be random. Have a plan.

Keep your eye on the road. That's where you will find the stars shining bright, even if you're not in Texas.

SPIRITUAL STRETCH #2: The first part of this Inspiration Destination is about *doing*. Nothing is more practical than a step-by-step plan! This part is about *thinking*. Consider *why* you want to be more inspired.

Do you just want to "feel good"? Do you want to be authentic? Are you searching for a sense of new or regained meaning?

Also, how do you feel about this entire exercise? Are you a "planner"? Do "planning" and "goals" seem disconnected from "inspiration" for you? Why? Does it make sense to you? Why?

Journal about your feelings regarding your roadmap to a destination of inspiration. How can you get excited about this? What is in it for you? For your team? Your patients?

CHAPTER 23

INSPIRATION DESTINATION:
WRITE A LETTER FROM YOU TO YOU

MY OWN BEST FRIEND

Have you ever heard the expression "You're your own worst enemy"?
I don't know about you, but I have had this quoted to me more than a
few times in my life.

I tend to be pretty hard on myself and sometimes it has led me to spiral
into insecurity and self-doubt. Sometimes, even when faced with over-
whelmingly *good* odds, I have completely convinced myself that I would
fail, and many times I did.

Many good friends and wise mentors have looked me in the eye and
said, "You're your own worst enemy." I resented them for that. How dare
they blame me for my own life circumstance! Didn't they know that it
wasn't my fault? I was a victim! Poor me.

You know, it has also been said that "denial isn't just a river in Egypt." I
was having a really difficult time facing the fact that I was creating some
of my challenges. I was having some tough times midway through my

nursing life. I was struggling with where I wanted to go. I felt as if I had lost my passion. I was dragging. I was going through the motions.

Honestly, when I look back, I was hurting. I sought help from friends and professional mentors. I knew what was coming: the "worst enemy" speech. After one such talking to and a subsequent trip to denial, I had a thought. There is an opposite to everything. Good has bad. Dark has light. Hot has cold. So wouldn't "enemy" have as its opposite "friend"? If you could be your own worst enemy, could you also be your own best friend?

It made sense to me. So right then and there, I stopped beating myself up like a sad piñata at a pity party and sat down to think about what it would mean if I were "my own best friend." I wrote a couple of things down in my journal. I started off by writing: "If I were my own best friend..."

Some of it went like this:

> "If I were my own best friend, I would tell myself what a difference I make in the lives of the people who trust me with their care. If I were my own best friend, I would thank me for the lives that I have saved, the tears that I have dried, the IVs I have started on the first stick, and the children I have made giggle while they lay in hospital beds.

> "If I were my own best friend, I would be proud of the personal and professional obstacles I have overcome to get where I am now. If I were my own best friend, I would believe in my abilities to be the best, but I would give myself permission to seek progress before perfection.

"If I were my own best friend, I would encourage myself to learn from my mistakes rather than tell myself that my mistakes were the definition of who I am. If I were my own best friend, I would remind myself that each day is an opportunity to make the journey to love, joy, and inspiration—and that I have the power to punch that ticket.

"If I were my own best friend, I would never put myself down or speak disrespectfully of myself or to myself. I would use words of encouragement, love, support, and friendship. I would lift myself up, not out of conceit or self-importance but out of the firm belief that I was put here to make a difference and that the work I do has great purpose. If I were my own best friend, I would forgive myself for my flaws and I would encourage myself to be quiet, meditate, and pray for peace and wisdom.

"If I were my own best friend, I would tell myself that being inspired is not self-serving but allows me to serve others from a place of authenticity and strength. If I were my own best friend, I would remind myself to be grateful, for I have been blessed a million times over to be on this journey, and I would have it no other way."

INSPIRATION DESTINATION: WRITE A LETTER FROM YOU TO YOU.

When I wrote that to myself it was transformational for me. I felt as if the "future" me was encouraging the "old" me. In a weird way, it gave me hope because it created for me the reality of a "me" that was inspired. I started down a road I had not been on for a long time. It probably saved my life in many ways.

You have read this far. Perhaps you have gone through these Inspiration Destinations and are in a better place than you were when you started. Maybe you read straight through and are deciding how to use them. Maybe you skipped right to the last chapter to see how the book ended! Either way, here we are.

Thank you.

Thank you for caring enough about yourself, your team, and your patients to want to be more inspired. Thank you for wanting to increase the passion you have for the amazing work that you do. I know that when you are more inspired, you will bring more light to your world. That light will shine on many people.

You will be a new nurse. You will be a difference-maker like never before. Being an inspired nurse will allow you to do great things. I am convinced of that. My hope is that what you have read, felt, and done while experiencing this book has encouraged you along this journey to inspiration. My great hope is that you will be an inspiration to others.

So now we have one last Inspiration Destination. Today, you are going to write a letter. You are going to need to use some imagination here. I want you to pretend that you are writing a letter to someone you love very, very much. This person has done amazing work in her nursing career. She is deserving of hope.

You believe in this person and you want her to be uplifted. This person is your very best friend. How would you encourage her? What pearls of wisdom and inspiration could you pass along to her? What would your words of sage advice be?

This person you are writing this letter to is, of course, *you*. Take your time. Be in a place where you can be quiet. You need to really nurture this person. She needs you. Her life depends on it.

Take this seriously. What would you say to yourself if you were your own best friend? What would you want to hear from someone who loved you with all of her heart? You can use the format I used above in my own letter or another format that suits you. Whatever works for you.

When you are done writing this letter, put it in an envelope, address it to yourself, stick a stamp on it, and mail it to yourself.

In a day or two you will get the letter in the mail. Take it to a quiet place and read it. Let the words sink in to your mind. They are your words, but you will notice that they somehow seem different. Appreciate the wisdom that is inside of you. You will find that you know yourself better than you thought.

Keep that letter someplace special. You may need it from time to time. Know in your heart that this is who you are. The wonderful, amazing, inspirational nurse that you are lifting up is *you*. Let that sink in.

That is where inspiration lives. It comes from inside—that's why it is not called "outspiration"!

Experience what it would be like to be your own best friend.

We started this journey talking about a question. I hope you found some answers in these pages. I hope you laughed and even cried. It is good to feel that passionate. I hope that some of these stories reminded you of some of your own.

I am grateful for the lessons that I have learned, and I am grateful to have had the opportunity to share them with you. I am still learning. I have so much yet to learn. I have so very far yet to go. That's okay. This is a journey.

I am inspired by what I have seen loving and brilliant people do throughout my whole career. People like you. I stand in reverence of the patients and fellow healthcare givers who reach heights of inspiration that I have not yet seen but hope someday to glimpse.

You asked the question, "Can I feel better about my nursing journey?"
The answer is, "Yes."
You asked the question, "Can I regain a sense of purpose, authenticity, and meaning in my nursing walk?"
The answer is, "Yes."
You asked the question, "Can I be an inspired nurse?"
The answer is, "Yes."
It was always "yes."

It's good to ask questions. It is, after all, what smart people do.

ACKNOWLEDGMENTS

I would like to thank the following:

All of Studer Group's PRC's, coaches, speakers, leaders, and employees for your friendship, support, teaching, and hard work. You make such a difference.

Cassie Henze for your artistic eye and talent.

Dottie DeHart and team for your patient editing.

Dan Collard for mentoring and coaching.

Nick Tamposi at P Model Management. You literally made me look good.

Stacy Tompkins, you rock!

Dr. Kathryn Keller, PhD, MSN, for your fantastic review and advice.

David Zambrana for being my "brother from another mother."

Karen, Tom, Kelly, RT, Joe, and Leslie for your friendship.

Fr. Julian Harris and Fr. Alex Vargas for your prayers, friendship, and example.

The Bluni and Bonelli families for their love.

My big brothers, Jack and Bob, I love you both.

My mom, Ann, thanks for watching the clouds with me. I love you.

My dad, Jack, I miss you.

My mother-in-law, Vickie, thanks for all that you give. I love you.

My partners, past and present, especially Heartland Health in St. Joseph, MO, Nemours Children's Hospitals and Clinics, University of Miami, OMHS, MUSC, Baylor and Memorial Health, you are all incredible.

My friends at Delray and Tenet.

The entire team at Holtz Children's Hospital, especially the PICU and the Jackson Memorial Hospital Ryder Trauma Center TICU in Miami, thanks for your daily miracles.

Dawn for being amazingly supportive, beautiful, wonderful, and every other good adjective that exists. I love you so much.

Luke, I love you already.

Rhett Bluni for being the coolest kid ever.

Craig Deao for being the funniest person I know.

Brian Robinson for wisdom and encouragement.

BG Porter for being the best example of a company president that there is. Your leadership is inspiring. I am grateful to work for you.

Bekki Kennedy for all of your hard work, great spirit, creativity, faith, and brilliance. Thank you.

Quint Studer for having the vision, passion, inspiration, and soul to create Studer Group. I am a better person because of you. Healthcare is truly a more inspirational place because of you.

INSPIRED TO GIVE
(A WORD FROM RICH BLUNI, RN)

If you purchased the book you're holding, thank you. A portion of the money you spent will be donated to the Pediatric Intensive Care Unit (PICU) at Holtz Children's Hospital in Miami, Florida. Also called the "Carnival Cares for Kids Center"—and affiliated with Jackson Memorial Hospital—it is a regional resource for the care of critically ill children.

Approximately 1,000 patients from throughout Florida and the Caribbean region—ranging in age from infancy to 21 years—are admitted here annually. This state-of-the-art unit, which receives medical, surgical, and trauma patients, features oversized rooms that allow families to comfortably stay overnight with their children.

I worked as an RN in this unit for more than five years. It was the hardest job I ever had, and the most inspirational. The nurses and physicians working there performed miracles every day. Their level of commitment to children and the families who love them is nothing short of amazing.

Because I learned so much from Holtz about what it means to be a nurse, I wanted to give something back. In fact, I felt called to do so. I take the PICU and the experiences I had there with me wherever I go. They are a part of me. And I am grateful that together, through this book, we can contribute in some small way to the healing of children yet to come.

ABOUT THE AUTHOR

Rich Bluni, RN, is a national speaker and coach for Studer Group®, but the title of which he is proudest is "Nurse." An RN since 1993, he chose the profession after seeing the tremendous impact nurses had on his father after he was diagnosed with terminal cancer.

"I saw the great and small things nurses accomplished in their day and realized that there was no higher calling, for me, than to become a nurse," he says.

Rich has worked in Adolescent Oncology, Pediatric ICU, and Trauma ICU departments as well as serving as a Pedi flight and transport nurse. A Licensed Healthcare Risk Manager, he has served as ED Nursing Manager and Director of Risk Management and Patient Safety.

In 2008, he won the Studer Group Pillar Award, which is given for achievement of outstanding outcomes.

Rich and his wife, a nursing professor and former ED and Trauma nurse, live in Boynton Beach, Florida. His son Rhett is the greatest joy in his life. Today, Rich works to improve patient outcomes and encourage the spirits of nurses and all healthcare professionals who've answered the calling to serve others with their hands and hearts.

ADDITIONAL RESOURCES

Accelerate the momentum of your Healthcare Flywheel^{SM}.
Access additional resources at www.studergroup.com/inspirednurse.

Books:

Hardwiring Excellence—In _Hardwiring Excellence_, Quint Studer helps healthcare professionals to rekindle the flame and offers a roadmap to creating and sustaining a culture of service and operational excellence that drives bottom-line results.

What's Right in Health Care: 365 Stories—This 742 page book shares a story a day submitted by your friends and colleagues. It is a daily reminder about why we answered this calling and why we stay with it—to serve a purpose, to do worthwhile work, and to make a difference.

Results That Last—Healthcare leaders typically read "general business" books and figure out how to apply them to a healthcare setting. Quint's book _Results That Last_ represents a unique opportunity to share the tremendous progress our industry is making with leaders in other business arenas.

CDs:

Passion & Purpose, a new CD featuring The Calling, speaks of the journey of those who are drawn to make a difference. To order, visit www.studergroup.com.

Studer Group® Institutes:

Whether your healthcare organization is just starting its journey to implementing a culture of excellence, or it is looking to create change in a specific area, Studer Group Institutes offer a range of learning opportunity.

<u>Taking You and Your Organization to the Next Level</u>—Learn the tools, tactics, and strategies that are needed to *Take You and Your Organization to the Next Level* at this two-day institute with Quint Studer and Studer Group's Coach Experts. You will walk away with Evidence-Based Leadership^{SM} strategies to create a sustainable culture of execution.

<u>What's Right in Health Care</u>^{SM}—One of the largest healthcare peer-to-peer learning conferences in the nation, *What's Right in Health Care* brings individuals together to share ideas that have been proven to make healthcare better.

Reignite your flame by attending any of Studer Group's passion-driven institutes. Nursing Contact Hours are awarded at each institute. Visit www.studergroup.com/institutes to view a list of upcoming institutes.

To view a list of the Nurse Contact Hours we offer for each institute, visit www.studergroup.com/CMEcredits.

Studer Group Patient Safety Toolkit:

Nothing is more foundational to our patients or to us as healthcare professionals than ensuring that patients receive safe care.

In this toolkit, we describe how specific, hardwired behaviors can be applied to patient safety. By using the same tools to improve patient safety that have already been proven to achieve clinical, operational, and service excellence, your organization will save time, expenses, and most importantly, lives. For more information on the Patient Safety Toolkit, visit www.studergroup.com.

Speakers:

Studer Group provides speaking engagements for healthcare organizations all over the country. These speakers began their lives in healthcare for many reasons, but the main reason was to make a difference in the lives of others.

Rich Bluni, RN, Studer Group National Speaker
Rich Bluni, RN, the author of *Inspired Nurse*, rates on average a *4.95 out of a 5.0* scale at his speaking engagements. Rich has more than fourteen years of clinical, legal, risk management, patient safety, and nursing management experience, and when Rich presents on stage, he brings all of his experiences to life!

To view Rich Bluni in action or to gather more information on Studer Group national speakers, visit www.studergroup.com/speakers.

Learning Videos:

AIDET^{SM} Five Fundamentals of Patient Communication
AIDET—Acknowledge, Introduce, Duration, Explanation, and Thank You—is a powerful communication tool. When interacting with patients, gaining trust is essential for obtaining patient compliance and improving clinical outcomes. AIDET is a comprehensive training tool that will enhance communication within your organization.

Hourly Rounding
Improving Nursing and Patient Care Excellence—A Studer Group Patient Care Model and video/DVD training that contains a key strategy we call hourly rounding. Hourly rounding is not only a call light reduction strategy, but also a proven tactic to reduce patient falls by 50 percent, reduce skin breakdowns by 14 percent, and improve patient satisfaction scores an average of 12 mean points.

Must Haves® Video Series
By implementing the Must Haves, healthcare organizations around the country are seeing better bottom-line results, including increased volume and decreased length of stay, as well as improved clinical outcomes, staff retention, and recruitment. The Must Haves video series consists of live lectures by Quint Studer, followed by role plays to help organizations hardwire these breakthrough practices into their culture.

Visit www.studergroup.com to view additional learning videos.

Magazines:

Hardwired Results Issue 1 Fall 2004
This issue focuses on employee loyalty. Article topics include rounding for outcomes, the power of thank you notes, a case study of Delnor Community Hospital, and a leadership self-test.

Hardwired Results Issue 7 Fall 2006
This issue features articles and tools to drive outcomes. Learn how to improve clinical outcomes with hourly rounding and increase patient satisfaction with individualized patient care.

Visit www.studergroup.com to view additional *Hardwired Results* magazines.

Webinars:

Studer Group webinars provide the latest information and tools on topics critical to healthcare leaders. Presented by Quint and other Studer Group coaches, each "on demand" webinar is an hour long. Participants will receive handouts and the opportunity to purchase the webinar on CD to teach other leaders in their organizations.

Visit www.studergroup.com to learn more about the webinars that are available.

ABOUT STUDER GROUP

Studer Group is an outcomes-based healthcare consulting firm devoted to teaching evidence-based tools and processes that organizations can immediately use to create and sustain outcomes in service and operational excellence. Partner organizations see clear results in the areas of higher employee retention, greater patient and customer satisfaction, healthy financials, growing market share, and improvements in various other quality indicators. Studer Group has worked with hundreds of health care systems, hospitals, and medical groups since the firm's inception in 1999 and additionally is operating in Canada, Australia, and New Zealand.

<u>Mission and Vision</u> Studer Group's mission is to make healthcare a better place for employees to work, physicians to practice medicine, and patients to receive care. Our vision is to be the intellectual resource for healthcare professionals, combining passion with prescriptive actions and tools, to maximize human potential within each organization and healthcare as a whole.

<u>Harvesting Best Practices from a National Learning Lab</u> CEO Quint Studer and Studer Group's coaches teach, train, and speak to thousands of leaders at healthcare organizations worldwide each week, both on-site through coaching engagements and at frequent industry speaking engagements. This ongoing "in the trenches" dialogue provides ample opportunity to spot best practices in action from "first mover" innovators at many organizations. These are then harvested and tested in other organizations, refined, and shared with all healthcare organizations

through peer-reviewed journal articles, Studer Group publications, and products to accelerate change.

Because we find that reducing leadership variance lies at the very heart of creating a consistent culture of excellence, Studer Group also helps organizations to hardwire great leadership. The firm retains a specialist to harvest effective tools and techniques and then share best practices for development of Leadership Development Institutes that efficiently turn training into results.

In July 2004, Studer Group also announced its Alliance for Health Care Research, which studies best practices using data from Studer Group's national learning lab to validate and quantify their impact and application at all healthcare organizations. The Alliance conducts rigorous qualitative and quantitative studies and invites participation by both client partners and non-partners of Studer Group.

Resources to Support Learning Studer Group's core values (teamwork, respect, integrity, generosity, and learning) are reflected in the products and services we offer. The Studer Group website, www.studergroup. com, offers a wealth of free information, articles, custom advice, and downloadable tools at no charge.

HOW TO ORDER ADDITIONAL COPIES OF

Inspired Nurse and *Inspired Journal*

Orders may be placed:

Online at:
www.firestarterpublishing.com
www.studergroup.com

By phone at: 866-354-3473

By mail at: Fire Starter Publishing
913 Gulf Breeze Parkway, Suite 6
Gulf Breeze, FL 32561

(Bulk discounts are available.)

Inspired Nurse and *Inspired Journal*
are also available online at www.amazon.com.